T0301811

SINGAPORE and HONG KONG

Comparative Perspectives

*On the 20th Anniversary of
Hong Kong's Handover to China*

SINGAPORE
and
HONG KONG
Comparative Perspectives

On the 20th Anniversary of
Hong Kong's Handover to China

Edited by
Institute of Advanced Studies
NTU, Singapore

World Scientific

NEW JERSEY · LONDON · SINGAPORE · BEIJING · SHANGHAI · HONG KONG · TAIPEI · CHENNAI · TOKYO

Published by

Institute of Advanced Studies
Nanyang Technological University
60 Nanyang View
Singapore 639673

and

World Scientific Publishing Co. Pte. Ltd.
5 Toh Tuck Link, Singapore 596224
USA office: 27 Warren Street, Suite 401-402, Hackensack, NJ 07601
UK office: 57 Shelton Street, Covent Garden, London WC2H 9HE

Library of Congress Cataloging-in-Publication Data
Names: Nanyang Technological University. Institute of Advanced Studies, sponsoring body.
Title: Singapore and Hong Kong : comparative perspectives on the
    20th anniversary of Hong Kong's handover to China /
    Institute of Advanced Studies, Nanyang Technological University.
Description: Hackensack, NJ : World Scientific, 2019.
Identifiers: LCCN 2018054012 | ISBN 9789813237926
Subjects: LCSH: Hong Kong (China)--Economic conditions--21st century. |
    Hong Kong (China)--Politics and government--1997– | Hong Kong (China)--
    Social conditions--21st century. | Singapore--Economic conditions--21st century. |
    Singapore--Politics and government--1990- | Singapore--Social conditions--21st century.
Classification: LCC HC470.3 .S56 2019 | DDC 951.2506--dc23
LC record available at https://lccn.loc.gov/2018054012

British Library Cataloguing-in-Publication Data
A catalogue record for this book is available from the British Library.

For any available supplementary material, please visit
https://www.worldscientific.com/worldscibooks/10.1142/10931#t=suppl

Desk Editor: Tan Boon Hui

Typeset by Stallion Press
Email: enquiries@stallionpress.com

Printed in Singapore

Foreword

Hong Kong and Singapore are port cities sharing similar backgrounds. Both are former colonies within the British empire whose strategic geographical locations enabled their development as major regional hubs and inevitable rivals in many sectors.

In the 21st century, both are pursuing innovation-driven growth, but their political environments are increasingly divergent. Hong Kong celebrated its 20th year as a Special Administrative Region in China in 2017, while Singapore marked 50 years of nationhood in 2015. In the international arena, Hong Kong has effectively become part of China whereas Singapore still carefully negotiates its way as an island state.

On 4 September 2017, experts were invited to provide up-to-date insights on the post-colonial development of Singapore and Hong Kong, at the "Singapore and Hong Kong: Comparative Perspective on the Occasion of the 20th Anniversary of the Handover" workshop. This book is based on the keynote speeches of the workshop, that compares their development models in the political, economic and cultural domains. Leveraging on the comparative perspectives, it aims to map the prospects of these global metropolises and project their development in the next decade.

Phua Kok Khoo
Founding Director Emeritus
Institute of Advanced Studies
Nanyang Technological University

Adjunct Professor
Department of Physics
National University of Singapore

Contents

Singapore and Hong Kong:

Historical Images*

WANG Gungwu

 **Professor WANG Gungwu** is University Professor at National University of Singapore; Chairman of ISEAS — Yusof Ishak Institute. His recent books include *Renewal: The Chinese State and New Global History* (2013); and *Another China Cycle: Committing to Reform* (2014). His dialogues on world history with Ooi Kee Beng were published as *The Eurasian Core and Its Edges* (2015). *Home is not here* (2018) and *Nanyang: Essays on Heritage* (2018). And in Chinese《华人与中国：王赓武自选集》(2013) and《天下华人》(2016). He received his B.A. and M.A. from University of Malaya in Singapore; and his Ph.D. from SOAS, London. From 1986 to 1995, he was Vice-Chancellor of University of Hong Kong.

Many people have compared Hong Kong and Singapore directly or indirectly over the past century. Innumerable books, articles, and commentaries have been published, especially during the past few decades. The 20th anniversary of Hong Kong's return to China provides a good reason to

* This is the revised transcript of a lecture given to the workshop "Singapore and Hong Kong: Comparative Perspective on the Occasion of the Handover" held on 4 September 2017, in Singapore.

look again and compare the Special Autonomous Region with Singapore after its fifty years of independence. Although the two cities started as British colonies one after the other at the peak of imperial expansion early in the 19th century, they have had different trajectories of development. Here, I am reminded of two reference points.

In 1970, five years after the independence of Singapore, when Hong Kong was still in the shadow of The People's Republic of China's Great Proletarian Cultural Revolution, the University of Hong Kong awarded an honorary degree to Prime Minister Lee Kuan Yew. He highlighted the different futures that faced the peoples of the two cities by choosing to speak on "A Tale of Two Cities". In 1992, as Vice-Chancellor of Hong Kong University, I invited Mr Lee to come again to speak on the Two Cities Revisited. He willingly agreed and gave us a cogent analysis of the similarities and differences between the two cities since he last spoke.[1] Governor Chris Patten chaired the meeting in his capacity as Chancellor. He and Prime Minister Lee engaged in a lively discussion that included Singapore's membership in the Commonwealth as an independent republic as compared with Hong Kong's return to China.[2]

The contrasting fates were clear. However, I suggest that each city had a foundational theme in its history and shall focus here on why the respective themes have prepared each of them to play important roles in our region. My starting-point is that the two cities had a common history for almost 180 years. The British founded Hong Kong as a free port in 1840 after Singapore's foundation twenty years earlier and governed both cities by the same principles of colonial rule and administered them to serve the same imperial purpose. In addition, although located in the middle of the Malay world, Singapore became an entrepôt with a large Chinese majority, while Hong Kong was from the start populated by Chinese from China.

I first saw the two cities in 1936 on my way to China when I was six years old. We passed through Singapore and Hong Kong to go to Shanghai. I was awed by all three cities but it was Shanghai that caught my imagination. It stood out as a place that did not serve only one colonial power. The city's multicultural bright lights and glittering shows and theatres remained in my mind for years as did the name it boasted, "Pearl of the Orient", and its claims to serve the world in the Far East.

During the Second World War, the three cities went through hard times under Japanese occupation. I visited them again in 1947 and found them each displaying a mixture of decay and hope. Indeed, radical changes had taken place to all of them and more challenges were to come. After the communist takeover in 1949, Shanghai was wound down and critical assets were moved from there to Hong Kong. Within a few years, those transfers transformed Hong Kong into a city that integrated the best features of the two, a new "Shanghai-Hong Kong" that became a powerful metropolitan amalgam of great potential. This was also because the colony was a huge refuge for large numbers of entrepreneurial Chinese. The People's Republic of China could have taken the island by force but it decided that Hong Kong had qualities that China did not have and its people had skills invaluable for the new regime. Nevertheless, China made it clear that Hong Kong's decolonization would not be through independence, but by eventually returning to the motherland.

Singapore had a different transformation. Its leaders hoped for independence from Britain by becoming part of the Federation of Malaya. However, when Malaya became a nation-state in 1957, Singapore remained a colony. Afterwards, it did join the larger federation of Malaysia, but less than two years later, was once again separated to be an independent republic. Lee Kuan Yew's People's Action Party set out to build its own multiracial nation and, five years after that, he received his HKU honorary degree as its Prime Minister.

I was by then in Canberra at the Australian National University where I spent 18 years. During those years, I visited both Singapore and Hong Kong regularly and noted the differences in their developments. Unexpectedly, the opportunity came to move in 1986 to the University of Hong Kong. I found the pace of Hong Kong life overwhelming. The speed of all activities there was close to frenetic. Ten years later, when I came to Singapore, I experienced relief in the much quieter city where I found it possible to breathe normally. I actually needed some time to readjust to the slower pace. But, after living here for 22 years, I can say that Singapore has changed remarkably. The city has speeded up and, like it or not, it is in many respects becoming more like Hong Kong.

However, I continue to be struck by two very different constants in the history and development of the cities. Each draws on its particular location and the composition of its peoples. Here, I shall focus on these constants because I believe they represent divergent trajectories of change that make the story of the two cities more comprehensible.

For Singapore, the constant that defined much of the city's history is the idea of separation. This is not simply because Singapore was separated in 1965 from Malaysia, the event that enabled Singapore to become independent. What made that separation significant was that it marked the climax of a history that began in 1819 when the island was first separated from the Malay world. That was an ominous start. Up to that point, Singapore belonged to an evolving Malay seascape in which a wide range of peoples and ethnic groups had spread across maritime Southeast Asia and their connective experiences brought coherence to their lives on thousands of islands. The Malay peoples had by then developed a growing sense of identity and could be said to have had a shared history.

The British separated Singapore from that Malay world. Unlike in Penang, where they extended their jurisdiction to Province Wellesley on the mainland, here they concentrated on the island's goal of attracting a mercantile and cosmopolitan population to the port itself. When the Anglo-Dutch treaty was signed five years later in 1824, an additional dimension of being separate was extended northwards to include the whole length of the Straits of Malacca. In time, vestiges of the Malay past were submerged.

Singapore did have special relations with its immediate neighbour on the mainland, the state of Johor. But, for decades, relations with other Malay sultans on the peninsula were limited to investing and trading in products like tin, pepper and gambier. Separation was sustained by the legal and administrative structure that was erected to make the free port as appealing as possible. When Chinese from the neighbourhood as well as from South China came in larger numbers and became the majority people on the island, they did so because Singapore allowed them to operate under advantageous conditions.[3]

The colonial officials responded to the external separation experienced by each community by gradually adopting an inclusive policy for people within the colony. They had first followed convention by keeping the various communities apart. As the city grew, commercial needs minimized the barriers, but the tensions between business mixing and social distance remained. While each group of leaders was encouraged to work for communal harmony, separation remained the norm. A notable example was the work of the powerful institution of the Chinese Protectorate created to deal with the affairs of the Chinese majority.[4]

At another level, the British did reduce the effects of separation. In the interest of efficiency, they established closer connections among the ports under their control. Singapore became less separate when, in 1867, it was joined together with Malacca and Penang to form the Straits Settlements. There were also other forces that combined to reduce the sense of being apart. British power continued to expand following rapid advances in transport and communications technology. Economic opportunities drew the British more deeply into the Malay states on the peninsula. By the end of the 19th century, four of the sultanates were brought under their protection to form the Federated Malay States. Added to the special relations with the state of Johor, this made Singapore less distant and the colony took on more responsibilities for Malay affairs. When it was agreed with the King of Siam that four other Malay states in the north would come under British control, it became convenient to refer to the several agreements as steps leading to an entity called British Malaya. There was now the chance to build a single economy and the urge to centralize all matters pertaining to this "Malaya" became strong.[5] For at least two decades before the outbreak of the Second World War, debates continued between those who sought to end the mixed jurisdictions in order to ensure greater efficiency and security and those who favoured indirect rule through treaties with nominally sovereign Malay states. The issue remained unresolved when the Japanese expanded their East Asian Co-prosperity Sphere into Southeast Asia in December 1941.

The Japanese defeat of the British made it possible to conceive of a larger Malay-language-based state that the Japanese offered to help create as a way to overcome the previous Anglo-Dutch divisions. Had that state — based on the idea of Indonesia Raya — been established, it would have been a serious threat to the Malay sultanates on the peninsula. It did not come about because the Japanese were defeated. But, for Singapore, the Japanese plan did presage a new separation.

Within months after the start of the war, the Japanese came to control directly or indirectly almost all of Southeast Asia. The only exceptions were the parts of Burma where they continued to fight the allied forces down to 1945. When they captured Singapore in February 1942, they not only made Singapore the headquarters of their imperial project but also, with great pride, changed its name to *Syonan-to*, placing the city under Odachi Shigeo, a civilian mayor appointed from the Home Office in Tokyo who had a longer view of an empire's responsibilities. The name, "lighting up the south", celebrated the victory in the south, emphasising its achievement during the reign of Emperor Showa (Syowa), 1926–1989. This was the only place in Southeast Asia that had its name changed into Japanese.[6]

The decision to separate *Syonan* from the rest of Southeast Asia signified Japanese intentions to keep it as the strategic port of their new "empire". Elsewhere, they could claim that they were liberating local peoples from Western colonial rule, and preparing the Malay peoples for ultimate independence under Japanese tutelage. Singapore's future, however, was different. Its renaming was not casual or simply vainglorious. It indicated that the Japanese recognized the essential role that a separated Singapore played in Britain's global maritime empire and planned to have it perform a similar role for them.

Significantly, Singapore was not only separated from the Malay States but also from Malacca and Penang, the two other states of the Straits Settlements. That too was ominous. As it turned out, British officials in London drawing up plans for the time when the allies eventually defeated Japan and they returned to Malaya, also decided to put the Malay states together with Penang and Malacca and establish a new polity called the Malayan Union.[7] Singapore was not included but would remain a separate colony from where the British could manage their interests on the Malay peninsula and northern Borneo, and also be used to base their other strategic and economic activities in Southeast Asia.

This postwar plan might only have been temporary, quite different from what the Japanese had in mind and also different in purpose from the first separation in 1819 from the Malay world. But the idea that Singapore had qualities that marked it off as a unique place was there. Whatever the ultimate intentions, the assumption was that a further period of separation was an acceptable condition for the longer term.

The Malayan Union that the British tried to implement in 1946 failed because, in the eyes of the Malays, it gave political rights to too many

Chinese and Indians who had been brought to the Malay state only to serve British economic interests. The British knew that Singapore with its large Chinese population was not welcome to the Malay rulers. But it also suited the British to retain the strategic port for their use as long as they could. The Malays rejected the Union, but when they renegotiated the Federation of Malaya in 1948, they still did not want Singapore and both sides agreed to leave it out. And that remained Singapore's position when Malaya became independent in 1957. By that time, the people of Singapore also wanted independence and still hoped that they could achieve this by joining the Federation.

Singapore was ready to rejoin the world from which it had been separated from and there were people in Malaya who expected that Singapore would eventually become a constituent state. Thus there was a sense of relief when an acceptable formula was found. In 1961, Prime Minister Tunku Abdul Rahman agreed to the idea of a Greater Malaysia that would bring together all British "possessions" in the Malay world. This came about when the British realized that they had to leave and planned to have their territories put together in the larger federation. Singapore could now be included. The Malay leadership in Kuala Lumpur was still reluctant. Although people in Singapore also had their doubts, they accepted that, sooner or later, Singapore would have to join Malaya as one country. Mr Lee Kuan Yew and his People's Action Party saw that as inevitable.

However, when the time came, it turned out that the long history of separation was difficult to set aside. Its shadow hung over all the hard negotiations about merger between 1961 and 1963.[8] When the federation eventually came about, the disagreements continued and, less than two years after joining, Singapore dramatically separated to become an independent republic. The idea of separation thus remained a defining marker in the Singapore story.

Much of what the new Singapore state started with in 1965 derived from that separation. One key aspect was the nationalistic tensions growing between Chinese and Malays that had largely been dormant in British Malaya before the war. That was changed when the Japanese openly discriminated against the Chinese. From then on, it became more difficult to bring the two races together and it continued to be a serious problem when Singapore was once again separated.

Its leaders saw how most new nation-states empowered its dominant ethnic community at the expense of their minority citizens. They did not choose to follow that path simply because it had a Chinese majority population and resisted calls to make the country a Chinese-based nation-state. Instead, they adopted a plural society formula that worked for inclusiveness within the country and set out to treat every community equally. That policy might have led some of the country's Chinese to think that they were being separated from their cultural links with China. However, in order to avoid Singapore being seen as the centre of a "third" China,[9] it was a price that its leaders were prepared to pay.

They therefore concentrated on developing policies that made every citizen feel that Singapore was home. Laws were drawn up to counter any sense of being cut off from their ethnic roots. New standards of behaviour were set to fulfill the ideals of a country in which every community knew that it belonged. The mutual respect demanded of each community turned out to be achievable because, for nearly two centuries, people in Singapore had been learning to live with the cosmopolitan port's separateness in the region. Given that background, its leaders worked strenuously to refine the pluralist formula to ensure that an exceptional city-state could eventually be built.

It was remarkable how the republic accepted separation as its foundation starting point and made that into a source of resilience. After the twenty years' struggle for survival during the Cold War and threatening communal divisions, Singapore emerged as a model of national development with an inclusive cosmopolitan society that characterizes a global city. Its successes built the ecology of trust that has bolstered its capacity to be an active member of the ten-nation Association of Southeast Asian Nations, ASEAN. I believe that the way Singapore met the challenge of separations has prepared the state to serve the regional organization with confidence. This in turn enables it to become an indispensable partner when Hong Kong steps up to become a key node in China's Maritime Silk Road Initiative.

When asked to compare Hong Kong and Singapore today, I thought of the latter's separation and sought an equivalent constant in the history of Hong Kong. The colony of Hong Kong started the same way as Singapore when the British established a colonial administration and separated the island from China. However, Hong Kong's history of nearly 180 years suggests that there was no real separation. All the original inhabitants were Chinese and, throughout the time the British were in Hong Kong, the Hong Kong population was predominantly Chinese. Most of the newcomers arrived from across the Chinese border close by. Later, at different times, there were others who came from other parts of China, but almost all were Chinese.[10] And, as Britain took over parts of the mainland across the harbour in Kowloon, and later obtained a 99-year lease of the New Territories, there was virtually no distance between the colony and China.[11] Most of the time, there was also no question of separation from Chinese customs and family values. And one could see only minimal divergences in the way Hong Kong Chinese built their lives in the British colony.

What was more, after 1842, Chinese who went overseas to Southeast Asia, North America and Oceania came to use Hong Kong as their transit point on their way out or on the way home. For many, Hong Kong was their base for connecting with China. Although everyone was made aware that the colony was administered separately from China and by very different laws, those who made use of Hong Kong retained their strong cultural roots in China. Hong Kong entrepreneurs carried out their businesses affairs along lines more or less the same as those within China. Differences were superficial and most people were quick to adjust their methods to fit both jurisdictions.[12]

For Hong Kong people, therefore, separation was never uppermost in their minds. Instead, what they experienced throughout the years as a British colony was strikingly similar to what is expressed in the slogan, "one country two systems". I suggest that this captures the history of Hong Kong better than any other phrase that has been used to describe the city's development, and would go so far as to say that much of the political and economic life in Hong Kong has rested on this modern, albeit cryptic, slogan. When it was used in the 1980s to serve as a rallying-call to produce the happy ending that the British, Chinese and Hongkongers looked for when the time came for Hong Kong to be returned to the motherland, this seemed to describe what they could live with. But, although very few Chinese doubted that Hong Kong was part of China, it was never clear that the three sets of protagonists really agreed as to how the "two systems" should function. The slogan was thus cryptic because, whether used for Hong Kong history or seen in practice today, it has been difficult to pin down.[13] Certainly, at the handover in 1997, most people understood that a great deal would have to depend on the goodwill that would allow the two systems to perform efficiently.

The phrase was first endorsed by Deng Xiaoping as a way of opening up negotiations that would reconcile socialist China with the capitalist economies of Taiwan, Hong Kong and Macau. The Taiwanese were divided about what one country should mean, but the people of Hong Kong and Macau embraced it without difficulty and even thought the formula of "two systems" was ingenious. I suggest that the slogan was easy to accept because it described a subtle and undefined relationship that had been there ever since Hong Kong became a colony. What was new was first, the *formal* acceptance of parallel structures of governance and second, the 50-years timetable that Deng Xiaoping had added to the slogan. Whatever uncertainty there was on the streets and in the corridors of power seemed to have come from different expectations as to what the two new conditions would entail.

Let me go back to history. From the start, British officials and merchants in Hong Kong never expected that the Chinese there would look to Britain as their country. What they asserted was that these Chinese must obey the laws of a superior system and the Qing empire acknowledge the British right to demand that they do so. As it turned out, those conditions ensured that Hong Kong could become a place where its Chinese residents could hold different opinions from officialdom in China, one that could also serve as a site for dissent. Therefore, many of them learnt how to use the opportunities available to advance their interests, including their political causes. But, whatever they did concerning China, they acted as Chinese who were addressing problems in their country.

A striking example was that people who were anti-Manchu and against the Qing dynasty came freely to Hong Kong from the start.[14] Among them were those who supported the cause of *fan Qing fu Ming* (oppose the Qing to restore the Ming) and were organized to do that through their secret societies, the *Tian Di Hui* and its various branches. They were descended from people who never wanted to be ruled by the invaders from distant Manchuria whom they considered not Chinese.

Unlike in the north, where Manchu rule became more acceptable, Chinese in the south by and large did not accept the Qing as a legitimate dynasty and resisted the Manchus wherever and whenever they could.

The British were aware that many Chinese who came to Hong Kong were anti-Qing. They also noted that it was the Christian missionaries working out of Hong Kong who inspired the rebels that launched the Taiping Rebellion soon after the colony was established, and that many people in the colony supported them. They knew that when the rebels failed, many found refuge in Hong Kong and remained active there while others escaped abroad through the port.[15] Later, there were many others who found similar backing and sought safety in the city. Perhaps the most famous were Sun Yat Sen and his comrades who were not only nurtured in Hong Kong's schools, churches and associations, but also freely used the colony as their base to overthrow the regime in Beijing.[16]

An interesting example of historical continuity may be seen in the organization known as Zhigongtang 致公堂 or Zhigongdang (党). Many of the organizations that supported the 1911 Revolution came together in North America under the name of Zhigongtang/dang that is now one of the registered political parties in China. The clusters of secret societies that formed it had been active since the 18th century and their links to the Chinese overseas are well-known. Zhigongtang-connected groups supported Sun Yat-sen and his followers among the Chinese who came back from Southeast Asia, North America, Australasia and elsewhere. Their leaders helped to finance and arm those who were hostile to the policies of the Manchu Qing dynasty. After the early Republic was divided and China came to be dominated by ambitious northern warlords, their members were divided in their support for rival groups. In Hong Kong, some backed Sun Yat-sen's Kuomintang while others assisted a variety of local leaders, using the colony as a base for their partisan activities on the mainland.[17]

There were other kinds of opposition. For example, when the communist party was almost destroyed by the Kuomintang in Shanghai in the late 1920s, many surviving party members went to Hong Kong and Southeast Asia and some used Hong Kong as a base for setting up connections with the outside world. During most of the period from the 1920s to the 1940s, leading members of the Kuomintang and the Communists went to Hong Kong to present their different versions of Chinese political culture and used the media, the schools and other institutions there as sites for dissent.[18]

Interestingly, that continued to be so after the Communist victory in 1949. It was then the Kuomintang supporters who used Hong Kong as their base to oppose what was happening on the mainland. Many who left China after the collapse of the Nationalist government, as well as those who escaped to Hong Kong during the Cultural Revolution, had also fought against the Communist Party. At the least, most were unhappy with the regime and continued to express their dissatisfaction while living in Hong Kong.[19]

In the meantime, for reasons outside China's or Hong Kong's control, the colony became the East Asian frontline between the anti-communists and the communists. During the Cold War, Hong Kong acted like Berlin as a point of contact as well as a listening post between the superpower protagonists. The Americans and their British allies saw the strategic importance of Hong Kong for their cause and all those who were anti-Communists were quick to use Hong Kong for their purposes. Yet there was no question of separation. At one level, the official system may often look to London, but in practice, most Hong Kong Chinese looked elsewhere. In the mix of informal systems in operation, each with its own objectives, people largely focused on matters connected in one way or another to China.

Looking back at the many dissenters in Hong Kong history, most could be described as patriots. They became prominent not because they were against China but spoke and acted in opposition because they disagreed with some of the people who were running the country. They were proud to be Chinese and wanted China to become better than it was. "One country" was never in question.

What has been difficult is how "two systems" should be understood. In the 1980s, it was seen as an administrative device, a political formula that Deng Xiaoping first used to tempt Taiwan back into the fold. However, when applied to Hong Kong, it seemed to describe a deeper underlying reality. The phrase reflected the city's experience of never having been really separate from China but often providing a safe place for dissent. Many leaders in China always knew Hong Kong as a place where

Chinese people could think and act differently. Some even recognized that what could be done in Hong Kong was not always possible to do elsewhere in China, and there were ways of doing things there through experiments and disputations that China could learn from. All that explains why the slogan was well-received and welcomed. I suggest that most Hong Kong people found the slogan familiar and sensed that it was a vital part of their heritage.

With one country not in question, living with two systems would appear remarkably normal for people in both China and Hong Kong. The reality was an unacknowledged condition that served most people's needs. It underlined the city's freedoms that Hongkongers thought marked what was civilized and practical. However, leaders in China had never formally acknowledged that condition and there had never been a time-table. Therefore, great efforts were made before the handover to spell out how the two systems should be officially connected and what would need to be done over the next 50 years.

Given that new sets of people have taken over after 1997, retaining the framework with deep roots in past practice provided a good start. Hong Kong people have been remarkably skillful in devising solutions to difficult problems. The past twenty years tested that ingenuity. Many would say that the results have been mixed, but the determination to sustain and develop "two systems" is still strong. The city's heritage of legally-framed freedom ensures that its enterprising people, as well as the new talents it has continued to attract, can all actively participate in China's Belt and Road Initiative (BRI) that now offers further new opportunities. If China appreciates the finer points in Hong Kong's heritage and helps the two systems further evolve, the Special Autonomous Region (SAR) can certainly become the node for the BRI's maritime sectors. I have little doubt that its people are ready to seize the chance to demonstrate again what their freedoms can enable them to achieve.

Singapore's journey with separation is comparable to Hong Kong's creative management of a "one country two systems" duality. From being a link in the British imperial chain of ports, Singapore is now part of a strategic network for a globalized world. It achieved its present position by sweat and guile after several separations. But, having learnt how to deal with each of them, it is now in a position to take on new roles. That success since independence has enabled it to become active in the ASEAN framework. With economic growth shifting to the maritime economy of the Indo-Pacific and China and other Asian nations strongly supporting that development, its position between the two oceans will be increasingly important.

Hong Kong was meant, after the First Opium War, to take Singapore's place in providing a gateway to China's markets. But the concessions zone of Shanghai became the base for Western dominance in East Asia while Hong Kong was seen mainly as the *British* gateway to southern China. It was the communist victory in 1949 that enabled Hong Kong to become an open and efficient port that is vital to, and dependent on, China's growth and stability, and serve as China's financial and logistics centre. Now that China has embarked on its One Belt, One Road project, Hong Kong is the obvious starting point for the maritime initiatives. I believe that China understands the value of Hong Kong's two systems heritage and wants the city's venturesome entrepreneurs and professionals to find as quickly as possible the best roles that they can play.

Strategically connected between the Indian and Pacific Oceans, Singapore is an essential player in China's new initiative. Like Hong Kong, it has great capacity for commitment, concentrated effort, and forward thinking and planning. Its deep experience of being externally separate but inclusive within can be combined with Hong Kong's ability to manage its heritage of "two systems". Together, the two cities can help the region grow to be a powerful dynamo in the global economy.

Notes

1. Lee Kuan Yew, Speech at Honorary Graduates Congregation 1970, HKU Website, the Honorary Graduates' Speeches, 75th Congregation, "Hong Kong and Singapore — a Tale of Two Cities"; Lee Ka Shing Lecture by Mr Lee Kuan Yew, Senior Minister of Singapore at The University of Hong Kong, 14 December 1992, Ministerial Speeches, 16, no. 6 (November–December 1992), p. 5.

2. This was remembered in the following report, "…. In 1992, addressing a gathering of worthies at Hong Kong University, he subjected the new

Governor, Chris Patten, to a withering attack on his proposals for democratic reform. "I have never believed that democracy brings progress," he said. "I know it to have brought regression. I watch it year by year, and it need not have been thus." (*The Telegraph*, Obituary, 25 March 2015).

3. Song Ong Siang's *One Hundred Years' History of the Chinese in Singapore*. London: J. Murray, 1923 (reprinted with an introduction by Edwin Lee. Singapore: Oxford University Press, 1984), may be compared with Walter Makepeace, Gilbert E. Brooke and Roland Braddell (editors) *One Hundred Years of Singapore*. Two volumes. London: J. Murray, 1921 (reprinted with an introduction by C. M. Turnbull, Singapore: Oxford University Press, 1991).

4. Lee Poh Ping, *Chinese Society in Nineteenth Century Singapore*, Kuala Lumpur: Oxford University Press, 1978; Ng Siew Yoong, "The Chinese Protectorate in Singapore, 1877–1900", *Journal of Southeast Asian History*, vol. 2, no. 1, pp. 76–99.

5. Yeo Kim Wah, *Politics of Decentralization: Colonial Controversy in Malaya, 1920–1929*. Kuala Lumpur: Oxford University Press, 1982.

6. Akashi Yoji and Yoshimura Mako (editors), *New Perspectives on the Japanese Occupation in Malaya and Singapore, 1941–1945*. Singapore: NUS Press, 2008.

   Anthony Reid has pointed out that the Japanese did change the name of Batavia, but Jakarta was the town's original name. This name change to Syonan aroused considerable attention in Singapore when a museum associated with the war was to be renamed "Syonan Museum". Many people objected because of the bitter memories that the name brought of Japanese rule, especially among Chinese who remembered how they were targeted for discriminatory treatment; http://www.straitstimes.com/singapore/war-gallery-name-change-a-timeline

7. James de V. Allen, *The Malayan Union*. New Haven: Yale University Southeast Asian Studies, 1967; and Ariffin Omar, *Bangsa Melayu: Malay Concepts of Democracy and Community, 1945–1950*. Kuala Lumpur: Oxford University Press, 1993.

8. Two studies highlight some of the major issues of disagreement and show that they arose from the long period of separation. Tan Tai Yong, *Creating "Greater Malaysia": Decolonization and the Politics of Merger*, Singapore: Institute of Southeast Asian Studies, 2008; and Albert Lau, *A Moment of Anguish: Singapore in Malaysia and the Politics of Disengagement*. Singapore: Times Academic Press, 1998.

9. The "third China" projected by C.P. Fitzgerald, in his *The Third China: the Chinese Communities in South-East Asia* (Singapore: Donald Moore and Australian Institute for International Affairs, 1969), described the very opposite of what the Singapore government experienced with the separation. Instead, the title played up the image of connections among the overseas Chinese acting as a "fifth column" for China.

10. G. B. Endacott, *A History of Hong Kong*. London: Oxford University Press, 1958; and Tsai Jung-Fang, *Hong Kong in Chinese History: Community and Social Unrest in the British colony, 1842–1913*, New York: Columbia University Press, 1995; and John M. Carroll and Mark Chi-kwan (editors), *Critical Readings on the Modern History of Hong Kong*, Four volumes, Leiden: Brill, 2016.

11. Peter Wesley-Smith, *Unequal Treaty, 1898–1997: China, Great Britain and Hong Kong's New Territories*. Hong Kong: Oxford University Press, 1980.

12. Two studies by Elizabeth Sinn portray this story most convincingly: "Hong Kong as an In-between Place in the Chinese Diaspora, 1849–1939", in Donna R. Gabaccia and Dirk Hoerder, eds., *Connecting Seas and Connected Ocean Rims. Indian, Atlantic, and Pacific Oceans and China Seas Migrations from the 1830s to the 1930s*. Leiden and London: Brill, 2011, pp. 225–247; and Elizabeth Sinn, *Pacific Crossing: California Gold, Chinese Migration, and the Making of Hong Kong*. Hong Kong: Hong Kong University Press, 2013.

13. Johannes Chan and Yash Ghai (editors), *The Hong Kong Bill of Rights: a comparative approach*. Hong Kong: Butterworths Asia. 1993; Peter Wesley-Smith and Albert H. Y. Chen (editors), *The Basic Law and Hong Kong's future*. Hong Kong: Butterworths, 1988.

14. Ming K. Chan (editor), *Precarious Balance: Hong Kong between China and Britain, 1842–1992*. Armonk: M.E. Sharpe, 1994; Wang, Gungwu 王赓武. (editor) *Xianggang shi xinbian* 《香港史新编》 [Hong Kong History: New Perspectives], two volumes. Hong Kong: San Lian Publishing Co., 1997, and revised edition 2016.

15. Carl T. Smith, *Chinese Christians: Elites, Middlemen, and the Church in Hong Kong*. Hong Kong: Oxford University Press, 1985.

16. Wong, John Y. H. 黄宇和. *Sanshi-sui qian de Sun Zhongshan: Cuiheng, Tandao, Xianggang, 1866–1895* 《三十岁前的孙中山：翠亨、檀岛、香港，1866–1895》 [Sun Yat-sen Before the Age of Thirty]. Hong Kong: Chung Hua Publishing Company, 2011.

17. Chen, Min 陈民. *Zhongguo Zhigongdang* 《中国致公党》[China Party for Public Interest], four volumes. Beijing: *wenshi ziliao chubanshe* 文史资料出版社, 1981; and Feng, Ziyou 冯自由. *Geming yishi* 革命逸史 [An Informal History of Revolution], four volumes. Shanghai: Commercial Press, 1946.

18. Chan Lau Kit-ching, *From nothing to nothing: the Chinese Communist Movement and Hong Kong, 1921–1936.* London: Hurst & Company, 1999; Christine Loh, *Underground Front: the Communist Party in Hong Kong.* Hong Kong: Hong Kong University Press, 2010; Cindy Yik-yi Chu, *Chinese communists and Hong Kong capitalists, 1937–1997.* New York: Palgrave Macmillan, 2010.

19. Richard Hughes, *Borrowed Place, Borrowed Time: Hong Kong and its many faces.* London: Andre Deutsch, 1976; and Ding Jie 丁洁 *"Huaqiaoribao" yu Xianggang huaren shehui 1925–1995* 《"华侨日报"与香港华人社会 1925–1995》[Wah Kiu Yat Po (Overseas Chinese Daily News) and the Development of Chinese Society in Hong Kong, 1925–1995]. Hong Kong: San Lian Publishing Co., 2014.

Two Pearls on the Maritime Silk Road:

A Tale of Two Competing Cities: The Lion City is Leading, What Should Hong Kong Do?

Antony LEUNG

Mr. Antony LEUNG, former Financial Secretary of Hong Kong Special Administrative Region, is Group Chairman & CEO of Nan Fung Group, a leading regional conglomerate focusing on property & investment businesses. He is also Group Chairman & Co-Founder of New Frontier Group, a group that engages in health care, elderly services and investment business in China. Concurrently, Mr. Leung is Independent Non-Executive Director of China Merchants Bank, Chairman of two charity organisations — Heifer Hong Kong and Food Angel.

Mr. Leung also has extensive experience in financial services, including Chairman of Greater China of Blackstone, Chairman of Asia of JP Morgan Chase, Asia Head of Citi Private Bank, Regional Head of Citi Investment Bank, Treasury and Greater China. In addition, he was Independent Director of Industrial and Commercial Bank of China, China Mobile (Hong Kong) Limited, American International Assurance (Hong Kong) Limited, International Advisory Board Member of China Development Bank and Chairman of Harvard Business School

Association of Hong Kong. His past public service included Non-Official Member of the Executive Council, Chairman of Education Commission, Chairman of University Grants Committee, Member of Exchange Fund Advisory Committee, Director of Hong Kong Airport Authority and Hong Kong Futures Exchange, Member of the Preparatory Committee and Election Committee for the Hong Kong Special Administrative Region and Hong Kong Affairs Advisors.

It is always a difficult task to speak after Professor Wang (Wang Gungwu). It is an honour and pleasure to share my thoughts and views on Hong Kong mainly and a little bit on Singapore. I actually rarely speak outside of Hong Kong, but how can I turn down Dr Phua whom I have known for over 40 years and also the invitation from Principal Wang. Following what Principal Wang has said, I would just like to comment on two points, which in a way leads to the thesis that I am going to speak on.

The first one is on "one country, two systems" which Professor Wang so eloquently summarised as the competitive edge of Hong Kong. Hong Kong has always been, as Principal Wang said, one country. We always believe that we are part of China, but then we have two systems. Clearly, the question is what would happen after 2047, after the 50 years that was promised under the Basic Law. I would venture to say that as my own personal belief or at least a wish, I believe that (this is also aligned with the interests of) the central government of China would like Hong Kong to be successful under the "one country, two systems". It will be difficult to predict what will happen in 2047. However, if by then the "one country two systems" policy remains successful, meaning that Hong Kong remain a prosperous place, a place that can contribute to the growth of both Hong Kong and the mainland, I do not think there is any reason why the Central Government should turn it into "one country, one system". Afterall, how many countries in the world can have one country but have two systems to use? Such flexibility means that if situations requires, Hong Kong can be used to address the mainland's needs, while at the same time having an external window to the rest of the world. Why should China turn Hong Kong into "one country, one system" and lose such flexibility?

If we look back at history (obviously I am not a historian at all, and you will find that my presentation will focus mainly on the economy, which is a reflection of my background, as a banker and then financial secretary and now back in business again), in 1967 when Hong Kong had the so-called riots as described by colonial British or by the Chinese as "反英抗暴", meaning anti-British, it was a kind of revolt against a colonial government. Macau also had such so-called riot uprisings. I believe that the Portuguese government, and I was told that the British government as well, made the offer to the Chinese government, "Why don't you take back Hong Kong and Macau? We are not going to have such trouble." Zhou Enlai, at that point of time, the Chinese Premier, said "No, keep it." He ordered that the so-called uprising be scaled back because the Chinese government realised fully that they need a window to the rest of the world. Right now, one can claim that China is completely open and does not need a window to the world. However, on the other hand, no one can predict what the world's geopolitical situation is going to be like down the road.

Right now, we all can recognise that the unipolar world, which is dominated by a superpower, the United States (US), is moving to a multipolar world, which Professor Wang can probably attest to. In history, a multipolar world is usually not very stable. Hence, who knows whether Hong Kong's role as the window to the world will be useful again? If I were the Chinese government, I would leave it there as an option. Why give away the option? The critical question obviously is that in the next 30 years, can "one country, two systems" be successful? Successful to the extent that it will not cause problems for Beijing while Hong Kong continue to be prosperous and stable; as part of one country, yet retaining our core values, that we have our freedom, we are democratic, kind of equitable to all, and operate under the rule of common law? My thesis is that if we can achieve the above in the next 30 years, I believe it would be very likely that Beijing would continue to allow Hong Kong to operate under the "one country, two systems", which, as Professor Wang has said, has existed in Hong Kong for the last 200 years. So it is up to us in Hong Kong, i.e. the Hong Kong people, to make sure that "one country, two systems" will prove to be successful and useful, not just to Hong Kong people, but to the mainlanders as well.

On the role of Singapore, Professor Wang has said is a very useful maritime port, which applies to Hong Kong too. However, I believe with the high-speed rail, it may change that equation, though not 100%, over time. The high-speed rail now connects the Pacific Ocean to the Atlantic Ocean in a way that has never happened before. I remember former politicians and historians have said whoever controlled Eurasia would control the world. That was before the Americas were found and Eurasia was still a very large economy and the biggest landmass in the world. One of my friends who is the largest micromotor manufacturer in the world, has factories mostly located in Dongguan, in the southern part of China. He said that 70% of what he used to ship via the sea route is now going through the rail to Europe. I believe the high-speed train is going to change the landscape significantly. Hong Kong, as the former seaport and as the window to the world, will have to change and evolve. We can't just rely on being an entrepot or the only window of China to the rest of the world, as we were in the past. We must evolve and change into something else and that "something else" is really to develop ourselves as a metropolis, which is essentially what we call the Guangdong-Hong Kong-Macau Greater Bay Area.

In the Greater Bay Area, we do not just rely on trading with the rest of the world, but also providing value-add, including maintaining Hong Kong as a global financial centre, and hence enabling Hong Kong to continue to be the most important window of China to the world. The Greater Bay Area also has an edge in high value-added services and will help to improve the entire services sector and Chinese system in the area, to really improve its standards, in order to become a centre for ICE.

ICE stands for innovation, creativity and entrepreneurship. We already have a lot of very innovative companies in the world located in the Greater Bay Area, particularly in Shenzhen. We have the best manufacturing platform in the world. The Greater Bay Area can help Hong Kong to move forward if we can speed up the five flows — flow of people, flow of goods, flow of services, flow of information, flow of capital. That basically is my thesis. So now may I go back to what I have prepared, and I will try to do it fairly quickly.

Hong Kong and Singapore are really a tale of two cities. However, if I look back the last 20 years, at least based on one indicator, Singapore is leading. The question is what should Hong Kong do?

By GDP, Singapore has been growing faster than Hong Kong. It dipped a little bit recently, which I believe is because of the exchange rate (figure 1).

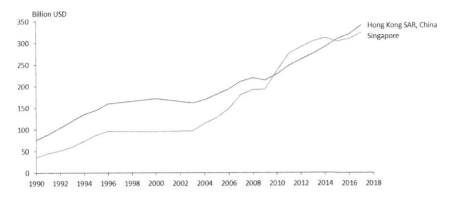

Figure 1   1990-2017 GDP, current USD

Source: World Bank

But then it is clear by the measurement of GDP per capita, Singapore is ahead. Why? More importantly, what should Hong Kong do? Though I am not qualified enough to talk about Singapore because I only lived here twice, the first time between 1980 and 1981, I was then the treasurer of Citibank in Singapore, treasurer meaning head of foreign exchange of money market. By the way, the money market and foreign exchange in Singapore in 1980 was more active and larger than that of Hong Kong, because the ACU-Asian Currency Unit was based in Singapore and not in Hong Kong. It was only later that Hong Kong took over, and now there is a tussle between the two, in terms of which one is more important as a financial centre. The second time I lived in Singapore was in 1996 when I was Citibank's head of private bank in Asia. But I had two offices both in Hong Kong as well as in Singapore, and I shuttled between the two places. So, I do know this city very well.

I am not going to go through the history, but suffice to say that the government here did a lot in investing for the future.

Hong Kong was the entrepot, the only international trade channel of China when China was closed. After China began to open, we shifted our manufacturing into China. When China took off after they entered World Trade Organization (WTO), Hong Kong benefitted as well from being its financial centre. Hong Kong's economy, you can say, emerges mainly because of China, but in a way, that was also a problem because we depended too much on China and became lazy, as I will explain later.

For Singapore, there are many success factors and you can summarize by saying that Singapore is successful because of the government. And obviously, the flipside is that, Hong Kong is successful despite the government. When China was closed and poor, Hong Kong was the only window, and when China opened, we stood to benefit because we were the window and conduct.

When Hong Kong was undergoing difficulties, China had grown stronger after the reform and opening up. China, being our motherland, was very good to Hong Kong. In 2002, Hong Kong was having trouble and unemployment was at 9%, as all the manufacturing sector activities went into the Mainland. At that time, I was the Financial Secretary. The obvious question to ask then was, which sector can employ a lot of lower-skilled workers. The answer was tourism. And so, we went to Beijing in October 2002 to ask for more tourists. Before that time, the mainland government did not really want Hong Kong to be overwhelmed by Chinese tourists, so they put a very tight lid on the number of tourists visiting Hong Kong. Tourists could only visit Hong Kong in group tours and the quota on the businessmen was two hundred thousand a year. When we said give us tourists, they said sure, and that was how tourism in Hong Kong took off. Subsequently, in June 2003, I represented Hong Kong in signing the Closer Economic Partnership Arrangement (CEPA) with the mainland, which some said was a signal that led to the economic return of Hong Kong to China.

I always say there are probably three different types of Hong Kong's return to China. The first one was the political sovereignty that happened on July 1st, 1997 when we had the exchange of flags. I was fortunate enough to be sitting on the stage. I was then a member of the Executive Council. It was a historic moment that I will never forget. However, economically, we were not as connected. With the signing of the CEPA, that signalled the economic return.

The return of the mind (人心的回归) is still going on, but why is Hong Kong lagging behind economically? Well, because we lost the monopoly (as China's window to the world) that we had. There was the trade percentage, we were a hundred and fifty percent, but now it is almost the same as Shanghai, since China entered WTO.

Our "total factor productivity" (TFP) didn't increase. Our population did not grow as fast, and more importantly, we did not invest enough in education, and our immigration policy was passive. Before the opening of China, a lot of the bachelors in Hong Kong could not afford to get married. After the opening up, these poorer Hong Kong people could then marry the poorer women in China. These people, together with their offspring, constituted part of the population growth in Hong Kong. Whereas in Singapore, the government deliberately recruited talents from around the world, particularly from the mainland. Together with the investment in education, in 1981 (I remember it was 1981 because I was in Singapore), Hong Kong's average education was more than that of Singapore. The situation reversed in 2011, with the average number of years of education of Singaporeans higher than that of Hong Kong citizens. So, the quality as well as the quantity of the workforce in Singapore improved significantly.

In Singapore, the government kept the housing price under control, whereas Hong Kong housing price reached to a level that is unjust. Today it takes 18 years of average family's income to buy an average-sized Hong Kong apartment, which is less than 500 square feet, so it makes Hong Kong uncompetitive. Whereas Singapore did the right thing by controlling housing prices. The government foresaw the changes in the world, promoted the higher value-added industries, and also attracted talents into Singapore. The Singapore Economic Development Board had been very aggressive and that was successful.

The Mainland of China was good to Hong Kong and is still good to Hong Kong. It gave us CEPA and all the tourists. When we can enjoy the low hanging fruit, there was no need to change. Also, the Hong Kong government believed in positive non-intervention policy (无为而治), which I did not believe in. When I was in the government, I said that the government's role should be a proactive enabler. But I was attacked all over by the local media as well as foreign economists, that we are abandoning the success formula for Hong Kong. I believe a positive non-intervention policy could be successful, but the qualifying condition is that the world has to be very stable, meaning the paradigms do not change. When the world is changing fast, and you are just repeating what you have done in the past, that may be the surest route to failure. After I left the Government, Hong Kong reverted to the positive non-intervention policy. With help from China, the unemployment went down to the current 3.2%. So why should the government do anything? And that to me is a mistake.

As I said Singapore is successful because of the government, Hong Kong in the past was successful despite the government.

One other current problem in Hong Kong is the large wealth inequality. Our Gini coefficient is 0.539, while for Singapore, it is only 0.458. The middle class is "sinking", and by the way, this is happening not just in Hong Kong, but the entire world. It happens not just because of Hong Kong's wrong policy, but because of globalisation and two other factors. One of which is new technology. New technology is eliminating jobs, not just from the lower class, but also from the middle class. I am predicting that not just drivers will be displaced, but also lawyers, investment bank analysts, auditors, and doctors. Right now, a lot of the earnings reports you are seeing in the newspapers are written by machines, not people. Artificial Intelligence can diagnose your illness much faster than a doctor. In Hong Kong, I have said before: when young people do not have the ability to "own decent housing" (上楼), "own upward mobility" (上流) and "to have their say" (上位), the only thing they can do is to "go onto the streets" to demonstrate (上街).

The most important problem that we are facing in Hong Kong is the lack of long term competitiveness. The service industry, which is our pride, is rigid, partly because the government regulations have not changed in time. Right now, what the government should do is deregulation (拆墙松绑), instead of just funding new projects.

"One Country, Two Systems" is our unique value to China. Whether we like it or not, China will be the largest economy in the world. Hong Kong should remain the most internationalised city in China. Under the two systems, we have the rule of law. We use English laws. We are the freest economy in the world, as testified by the Heritage Foundation for the last 23 years. We are multicultural, and we have low tax rates. And we are connecting with the rest of the world.

Our position? Very simple. We should be China's global talent centre as well as global financial centre. I have said in the past that Hong Kong should "ju rencai" (聚人才) and "ju qiancai" (聚钱财), meaning we should attract talent as well as attract capital, and talent (人才) is much more important than capital. So, this should be our role, we should attract talents, we should strengthen our status as an international financial centre, we should develop ICE (innovation, creativity and entrepreneurship), and provide various services to China.

Hong Kong has three strategic opportunities given to it: the Belt and Road Initiative, the Greater Bay Area, as well as the Renminbi internationalisation.

I am not going to say too much about the Belt and Road Initiative, because you know all about it. This is of epic importance, but it will take decades. It is an opportunity that can last for a long time. It is important because the supply-side formula such as improving the infrastructure and education would improve the economic growth of the poorer countries in the world, thereby narrowing the wealth gap between countries.

In terms of opportunities for us, the most obvious is in financial services. It takes a lot of money to build the infrastructure along the Belt and Road Initiative route. Some estimate that it will take US$8 trillion for infrastructure alone. The Asian Infrastructure Investment Bank (AIIB) can only provide part of it. The rest would have to be raised in the market. Hong Kong can provide financing not just in foreign currency or Hong Kong dollar, but also in offshore Renminbi. We also have all the other professional services that are needed.

Let's turn to the internationalisation of the Renminbi. As China grows, the Renminbi will be internationalised. It may present a threat to the US dollar but it is a must for China. On the other hand, the internationalisation of Renminbi doesn't mean that RMB has to be fully convertible at the capital account. If the convertibility barrier is taken away, we can be attacked by the speculators around the world, and we don't have the experience to counter that yet. China, I believe, will continue to internationalise the Renminbi but keep the capital account not fully convertible. This means that for a very long time, there will be two pools of Renminbi, onshore and offshore. There will be opportunities for Hong Kong because there needs to be connections between the two pools, risk management, as well as other derivative products and asset management products for the offshore pool. Hong Kong stands to gain because we are the largest centre for offshore Renminbi.

For the Greater Bay Area, the total GDP right now is US$1.3 trillion, quite close to the Tokyo-Osaka area which is US$1.8 trillion, and our growth rate is higher. Hong Kong, having "one country, two systems", is the financial centre with the freest economy, and we use the English law. Shenzhen is one of the most innovative cities in China. They already have Huawei and Tencent. These are global technology companies. And Dongguan and Shenzhen together have the world's best manufacturing platform, something that even the San Francisco Bay Area does not have. Zhuhai has plans to develop healthcare and biotech. If you combine all these, we are uniquely qualified to develop ICE.

This is a unique opportunity for Hong Kong and Guangdong if we can put all these together. Also, in China, among the three places — which are the Guangdong Greater Bay Area, the Shanghai Bay Area or the metropolis, as well as the Tianjin-Beijing Metropolis — The Bay Area, has the most number of top 100 universities in China, and most of them are in Hong Kong. If we are going to develop innovation, creativity and entrepreneurship, we will need all these top universities.

If we can somehow further improve the flows of people, goods, services, capital and information, as well as combine our research and development capabilities, we will be invincible.

To a certain extent, we are at the mouth of the "fengkou" (风口 or jet-streams). This is from a Chinese saying, "在风口面前，猪都会飞", meaning when the wind is strong enough, even a pig can fly. However, right now, one of the problems is that the "fengkou", the source of wind, is being blocked. The blockage is this: some of the young people in Hong Kong have become more inward-looking rather than outward-looking. Hong Kong, in the past, has always been very outward-looking. When there were not enough domestic opportunities, Hong Kong people went abroad. Many people in Singapore are originally from Hong Kong. Hong Kong people also went to other parts of Southeast Asia, with some going as far as Africa. However, right now, maybe the situation has changed, maybe life is too easy in Hong Kong. As a result, some of Hong Kong's young people will look for jobs in Hong Kong only. That is a kiss of death. To me, this is blocking the jet-stream. Hong Kong people can be outward-looking in the pursuit of the above opportunities (Belt and Road Initiative, RMB internationalisation and Greater Bay Area). We will not just be a pig, we can be an eagle and we can be soaring.

China, as I said, will become the largest economy in the world. It is going to benefit everybody, including Singapore. Mr Lee Kuan Yew, whom I have the utmost respect for, once said that if states and enterprises do not accept China's position and pay appropriate deference, they are faced with the threat of being shut out of a rapidly growing market with 1.3 billion people. I think it is worth repeating and remembering. Singapore should benefit from the rise of China. Singapore and Hong Kong should be the two shining pearls on the new silk road.

Hong Kong and Singapore:

No More Mirror Image of Each Other?

John WONG

Professor John WONG was former Professorial Fellow and Academic Advisor to the East Asian Institute (EAI) of the National University of Singapore. Prof Wong was formerly Research Director of EAI, and Director of the Institute of East Asian Political Economy (IEAPE). He taught Economics at the University of Hong Kong in 1966–1970 and at the National University of Singapore in 1971–1990.

He was a short-term academic visitor at the Fairbank Centre of Harvard University, Economic Growth Centre of Yale University, St. Antony College of Oxford University, and Economics Department of Stanford University. He held the ASEAN Chair at the University of Toronto.

He authored or edited 40 books, and published over 400 articles and papers on China, and development in East Asia and ASEAN. His first book, *Land Reform in the People's Republic of China* (New York, Praeger, 1973); and his most recent book, *Zhu Rongji and China's Economic Take-off* (London, Imperial College Press, 2016). In addition, he wrote numerous policy-related reports on development in China for the Singapore government. He obtained his Ph.D. from the University of London.

A Tale of Two Cities

In 1968, Singapore's Prime Minister Lee Kuan Yew, in his address at the University of Hong Kong's Honorary Degree Congregation, used the title "A Tale of Two Cities" to highlight the similarities and differences between the two city-based economies of Hong Kong and Singapore. Hong Kong was then a British Colony, but the only colony in modern history that was also rapidly industrialising. Singapore was then newly-independent and facing many problems of survival.

In the mid-1960s, both Hong Kong and Singapore were still developing economies with their per-capita GDP well below US$1,000, a level that was used to classify whether an economy is developed or developing. Singapore's per-capita GDP then was around US$700 while the colonial government in Hong Kong was reluctant even to collect economic statistics to compile a national income account. Hong Kong's Financial Secretary John Cowperthwaite (1961–1971), an ardent believer and practitioner of the *laissez-faire* policy, had openly declared his antipathy towards any economic and social statistics lest anyone used those statistics to question his policy of non-intervention.

Many decades later, both cities have successfully developed into high-income economies. For years, the two cities enjoyed largely the same level of per-capita GDP, with any small differences being mainly caused by exchange rate fluctuation, as the HK dollar has been (and still is today) closely pegged to the US dollar. By 2016, however, Singapore's per-capita GDP (nominal) reached US$52,960, compared to US$43,680 for Hong Kong, with Singapore's level higher than Hong Kong's by 21% as seen in Table 1. In PPP (purchasing power parity) terms, Singapore's GDP in 2016 amounted to $87,860, compared to Hong Kong's $58,550. Singapore's level is even higher, by 33%, in this measure.

This means that the income gap between Hong Kong and Singapore is not due to the exchange rate variation. Singapore's per-capita GDP in recent years is substantially higher than that of Hong Kong's, simply because the Singapore economy in this period has experienced higher economic growth. The Hong Kong economy has been so extensively de-industrialised during the past three decades as to become primarily a service-oriented economy. Hong Kong has therefore lost its former

Table 1   East Asia Performance Indicators

Countries	Population (Mn) 2016	GDP Per Capita (current US$) 2016	Total GDP (current US$, Bn) 2016	Growth of GDP (%)							
				1960–70	1970–80	1980–90	1990–2000	2000–2010	2014	2015	2016
China	1,378	8,123	11,199	5.2	5.5	10.3	9.7	10.3	7.3	6.9	6.7
Japan	126.9	38,894	4,939	10.9	4.3	4.1	1.3	1.1	0.3	1.2	1.0
South Korea	51.2	27,538	1,411	8.6	10.1	8.9	5.7	4.2	3.3	2.8	2.8
Taiwan*	23.5	22,540	531	9.2	9.7	7.9	5.7	3.9	4.0	0.7	1.5
Hong Kong	7.3	43,681	320	10	9.3	6.9	3.8	4.6	2.8	2.4	2.0
ASEAN-10											
Brunei	0.4	26,938	11.4	—	—	—	2.1	1.5	-2.3	-0.6	-2.5
Cambodia	15.8	1,269	20.0	—	—	—	6.4	7.9	7.1	7.0	6.9
Indonesia	261	3,570	932	3.9	7.2	6.1	3.8	5.2	5.0	4.9	5.0
Laos	6.8	2,353	15.9	—	—	—	6.1	7.1	7.6	7.3	7.0
Malaysia	31.2	9,502	296	6.5	7.9	5.3	6.5	5.5	6.0	5.0	4.2
Myanmar	52.9	1,275	67.4	—	—	—	6.1	10.8	8.0	7.3	6.5
Philippines	103	2,951	304	5.1	6.0	1.0	3.3	4.9	6.1	6.1	6.9
Singapore	5.6	52,960	296	8.8	8.3	6.7	7.4	5.9	3.6	1.9	2.0
Thailand	68.9	5,907	406	8.4	7.1	7.6	3.8	4.9	0.9	2.9	3.2
Vietnam	92.7	2,185	202	—	—	—	7.3	7.4	6.0	6.7	6.2
India	1,324	1,709	2,263	4.4	3.1	5.2	6.5	7.5	7.5	8.0	7.1

Source: World Bank.

* Taiwan data is obtained from CEIC.

Table 2   East Asia Social Indicators

	GDP per-capita (current US$) 2016	Total Fertility Rate (Births Per Woman) 2015	Life Expectancy At Birth 2015	Infant Mortality Rate (per 1,000 live births) 2015	Literacy Rate 15 Years & Older (%) Female 2005–15	Literacy Rate 15 Years & Older (%) Male 2005–15	Gross School Enrolment Ratio (%) Primary Female	Primary Male	Secondary Female	Secondary Male	Tertiary Female	Tertiary Male	Year	HDI 2015	Ranking 2015
China	8,123	1.6	76.0	9.2	93	98	104	104	96	93	47	40	2015	0.738	90
Japan	38,894	1.5	83.7	2.0	N.A	N.A	101	101	102	102	61	66	2014	0.903	17
South Korea	27,538	1.2	82.1	2.9	98	98	99	99	98	99	80	105	2015	0.901	18
Taiwan	22,540	1.2	80.2	4.0	97.3*	99*	99	98	N.A	N.A	88	80	2015	—	—
Hong Kong	43,681	1.2	84.2	2.0	N.A	N.A	110	112	99	103	74	64	2015	0.917	12
ASEAN-100															
Brunei	26,938	1.9	79.0	8.6	95	97	108	108	96	96	39	24	2015	0.865	30
Cambodia	1,269	2.6	68.8	24.6	66	83	116	117	N.A	N.A	12	14	2015	0.563	143
Indonesia	3,570	2.4	69.1	22.8	94	97	104	107	86	86	26	23	2015	0.689	113
Laos	2,353	2.9	66.6	50.7	63	83	109	114	59	64	17	17	2015	0.586	138
Malaysia	9,502	1.9	74.9	6.0	91	95	102	102	81	75	32	21	2015	0.789	59
Myanmar	1,275	2.2	66.1	39.5	91*	95*	98	101	52	51	15	12	2012–14	0.556	145
Philippines	2,951	2.9	68.3	22.2	97	96	117	117	93	84	40	31	2013–14	0.682	116
Singapore	52,960	1.2	83.2	2.1	95	99	101	101	108	109	95	85	2015	0.925	5
Thailand	5,907	1.5	74.6	10.5	92	95	99	106	125	133	57	41	2015	0.740	87
Vietnam	2,185	2.0	75.9	17.3	91	96	108	109	N.A	N.A	29	29	2015	0.683	115
India	1,709	2.4	68.3	37.9	59	79	115	103	75	74	27	27	2015	0.624	131

Human Development Index combines life expectancy, educational attainment and income indicators to give a composite measure of human development.
*Estimated value.

Sources: World Bank, World Development Report 2016, Asian Development Bank, www.data.gov.sg, Taiwan Ministry of Education, CIA Fact Book
Human Development Index combines life expectancy, educational attainment and income indicators to give a composite measure of human development.

dynamic source of economic growth associated with manufacturing activities — service activities, by nature, cannot grow very rapidly because of their inherent low productivity growth potential.

By comparison, Singapore's economic growth pattern has become much more broad-based as it still retains a sizeable manufacturing sector. In 2016, Singapore's manufacturing sector accounted for some 20% of its GDP as compared to Hong Kong's 1.5% while Singapore's service sector was only 74% as compared to Hong Kong's 93%. Furthermore, the Singapore government has been (until most recently) relentlessly pushing for higher economic growth with all available policy tools, including importing a large number of foreign labour, both high-skilled and low-skilled.

So Similar Then, More Different Now

Economically speaking, Hong Kong and Singapore are both complimentary and competitive. In some areas, they are very similar; and in others, they are very different. To begin with, both share a great deal of historical development experience and structural similarities. Both were former British colonies, thereby inheriting many common institutional features, from their legal system to their civil service. Both started off primarily as *entrepôt* economies, but were later forced to take to rapid industrialisation, because of political changes in their respective hinterlands and the need to cope with their high unemployment problem. Even their industrialisation strategies had similar characteristics. Both started off with labour-intensive industries, which were from the very beginning export-oriented, due to their small domestic markets. Driven by rising costs and increasing wages, both were later forced to restructure their economies by upgrading their industrial structure and going into higher value-added activities.

However, Hong Kong and Singapore started to follow different paths in their second lap of development on account of their different domestic policy environment and external circumstances. For Hong Kong, China's economic reform and open-door policy in the early 1980s provided a godsend opportunity for Hong Kong to accomplish its mission of industrial restructuring almost overnight, with its privately-owned enterprises conveniently shifting their labour-intensive industries across the border to

Guangdong, leaving Hong Kong to concentrate on service sector activities. Hong Kong often credits this smooth transition as the successful outcome of its time-honoured policy of "positive non-intervention", i.e. with little government involvement in the economic restructuring.

In contrast, Singapore's economic restructuring (called the "Second Industrial Revolution") has been much more protracted and also more difficult, despite state involvement and active government intervention. On the one hand, the government introduced a high-wage policy to put pressures on labour-intensive industries to restructure; and on the other hand, the government provided a lot of assistance to enterprises in the form of manpower training and state-supported R&D. Subsequently, the government, either through its government-linked companies (GLCs) or its various incentive packages and assistance, has continued to promote certain industries or to "lead" development towards a certain direction, from hi-tech electronics to pharmaceuticals and bio-tech industries, and from financial services to integrated resorts (the casinos). Government involvement also extended to Singapore's economic activities overseas (the "external wing" of the economy) through the setting up of industrial parks in the region.

In the area of social development, the Hong Kong government simply provides the financial resources to meet rising social needs. In Singapore, however, the government has been purposefully involved in its social policy formulation. In the early phase of Singapore's industrialisation, the government devoted a lot of its scarce financial resources to public housing and education while giving healthcare and social welfare a lower priority. This is because public housing (low-cost housing makes it possible for lower wages that are needed to make Singapore's exports more competitive) and education (human capital formation) were considered "investment" while healthcare spending (with a young population) and social welfare were mere "consumption", which did not directly serve economic growth.

Even in education spending, the government initially emphasised upgrading literacy and basic skills to cater for the labour-intensive phase of industrialisation, and hence, opened up more schools and technical training facilities. Subsequently, the focus was on the rapid expansion of science and engineering departments at the universities so as to support the industrial upgrading. Recent years have witnessed further expansion of post-graduate research and R&D facilities to dovetail with the development of the knowledge-based economy.

Suffice it to say that Hong Kong and Singapore have taken different paths to achieve their development objectives. Hong Kong's development is the successful outcome of its following the textbook case of the *laissez-faire* model. On the other hand, Singapore's development is also a success story of a "developmental state" model, a variant of the state capitalism development paradigm that has also been found in other parts of East Asia.

Still Lots of Similarities

The sharp contrast between Hong Kong and Singapore is best manifested in their political arenas. Hong Kong is the Special Administrative Region (SAR) of China, operating under the "One Country, Two Systems" model. Its long-term destiny lies in China, which also takes care of Hong Kong's security and defence. Singapore is an independent but a small city-state, always struggling to survive on its own. Whereas Hong Kong's hinterland supports its development and always stands ready to help out when it runs into difficulty, Singapore's hinterlands, by comparison, are not always friendly and supportive. To safeguard its independence, Singapore has to spend heavily on national defence — defence and security expenditure regularly eats up nearly 30% (used to be 40%) of Singapore's budget. It is indeed very costly for a small country like Singapore to maintain its independent statehood.

Beyond politics and foreign relations, Hong Kong and Singapore are actually sharing a lot of broadly similar challenges. As both are overcrowded urban enclaves with no natural resources, they have to continue to pursue pro-growth economic policies, and their peoples have to constantly work hard and remain highly entrepreneurial in order to "earn" their economic growth. Furthermore, both are open and outward-looking economies and hence highly exposed to external fluctuations from the global economy. And both economies are too small to generate sufficiently large domestic demand to offset the shortfall in external demand, as in China. Policy makers in both economies will have to be constantly on their toes, with a strong permanent sense of crisis. There are many roads leading to Rome. Ultimately, a good policy by a good government will always produce good results.

Socially speaking, both Hong Kong and Singapore have become a "developed society" with high levels of social development in terms of education, healthcare, life expectancy and so on. Both have made remarkable social progress in spite of the fact that the Singapore government has been more pro-active in the formation of its social policy. In fact, to the surprise of many, Hong Kong is performing better than Singapore in many areas of social welfare provisions. Apart from providing more generous public assistance to the poor, Hong Kong has recently also adopted the Minimum Wage Ordinance. The Singapore government, ideologically against any form of "state welfarism", has still not done this.

Nonetheless, both Hong Kong and Singapore, having achieved remarkable socio-economic progress, are now facing new sets of problems and challenges. There are admittedly many "cracks" in their respective development models, and rising income inequalities in both places (with their Gini ratios near 0.5) form just one example. There are also many burning issues that are crying out for attention. Both Hong Kong and Singapore have for years been facing the daunting challenge of a falling TFR (total fertility rate), which heralds the rapid ageing of the population. Both are also trying hard to cope with the social and economic ramifications of globalisation.

On October 12, 1968, Mr. Lee Kuan Yew, in his speech at the Hong Kong Correspondents Club, told his audience that the newly-independent Singapore was inspired by what Hong Kong did and how it overcame its domestic and external adversities. He started his speech as follows:

> Singapore is indebted to the example of Hong Kong. Three years ago, we were suddenly faced with a future on our own. Correspondents have explained how, through good fortune, hard work or enterprise, these years were about Singapore's best in terms of economic performance. But no one has mentioned an important factor, namely, Singapore's knowledge of the example of Hong Kong.

Five decades later, both economies and societies have matured, facing different sets of challenges. Singapore has just celebrated its 52nd anniversary of statehood, but still in process of transiting to the post-Lee Kuan Yew era. Hong Kong has recently elected its new Chief Secretary Carrie Lam, who is facing many new challenges including how to smoothly manage Hong Kong's integration with Mainland China under the "One Country, Two Systems" formula. Mr. Lee Kuan Yew used to believe that the Hong Kong people had the great capacity and ingenuity to overcome their adversity.

Problems and Challenges for Hong Kong and Singapore

KER Sin Tze

Professor KER Sin Tze taught at the Department of Economics & Statistics, the University of Singapore, during 1974-1980. He served subsequently as a Member of Parliament and Minister of State in the Singapore Government. He was also Trade Representative, Singapore Trade Office, Taipei, and Consul-General, Singapore Consulate in Hong Kong. He is now an Adjunct Professor at both National University of Singapore, and Nanyang Technological University.

Hong Kong celebrated the 20th anniversary of its return to China on 1 July 2017. Singapore celebrated its 52nd National Day on 9 August 2017. Both economies have grown at a respectable rate of around 2 percent in recent years. Their common challenge after Donald Trump became United States President is the anti-globalisation rhetoric which may threaten their economic survival and growth, as trade is important to both of them. Apart from globalisation, both have their own problems and challenges in the years ahead.

Hong Kong

1. *Lack of political support and long-term vision*

Under the Westminster parliamentary system, the Prime Minister has the support of Members of Parliament of his party in approving bills and implementing party policy. This has not been the case in Hong Kong. During the colonial administration, the governor had the executive-dominant power, and the appointed Legislative Council members were bound to support the governor. The central government recognised the merit of executive dominance of the colonial administration and decided to retain the same system. The purpose was to prevent excessive interferences by political parties on policy implementation, by strengthening the dominance of the Chief Executive, which was unfortunately unsuccessful. The reason is that Legislative Council members are mostly elected by voters, not appointed by the Chief Executive, and they are not bound to support him as in the colonial days.

The disassociation of the Chief Executive from political parties has led to the detachment between the Legislative Council and the Chief Executive. The Chief Executive Election Ordinance requires the winning candidate to declare that he is not a member of any political party. Its intention is to weaken the influence of political parties on the one hand, and to pre-empt any Chief Executive in claiming that he has the backing of his connected political party on the other hand, as this contravenes the dominance of the communist party. However, in actual practice, political parties' influence has been increasingly strong. After 1997, as mentioned earlier, the majority of Legislative Council members were elected by voters, not appointed by the government. Consequently, the detachment has caused the Chief Executive to lose political parties' support, making it difficult for him to get bills approved. Sometimes even the pro-establishment and pro-government parties have voted against government bills for populist support.

The detachment of political parties and the executive branch leads to a weak government, which inevitably lacks long term vision of policy implementation and governance. In a parliamentary democracy, political parties work out their party platforms in order to campaign for votes. The winning party forms the government and implements its policies based on its long term vision for the country. This is, however, not the case in Hong Kong. Political parties do not have the possibility of forming the government. Their role is mainly to scrutinise bills submitted for approval. As such, they do not need to have long-term vision and plan for the city. As Legislative Council members are now elected either from geographical constituencies or functional constituencies, they tend to be populists in garnering votes. Chief Executives and their teams do have their vision and plan for the city. However, due to the lack of support in the Legislature, Chief Executives often find it difficult to implement their policies. Moreover, they have been bogged down by many boycotts and protests. Under these circumstances, it is difficult for them to implement plans especially those with a long term vision.

2. *Universal suffrage*

In accordance with the Basic Law, the mini-constitution of Hong Kong, the Chief Executive is to be nominated and elected by an Election Committee which consists of representatives from commercial, professional, social and political sectors. Pro-democracy activists call this a "small circle election" and demand to replace it by universal suffrage. The pro-democracy camp also calls for the abolition of the 35 functional constituencies in the Legislative Council election, and demand all 70 seats by universal suffrage from geographical constituencies.

The subject of universal suffrage is not new. It was discussed in the drafting of the Basic Law. Under colonial rule, the Governor was appointed by the British Government and legislators were nominated by the Governor. There was no democratic election. But the British pushed for democratisation when they were departing from Hong Kong. As a result, Beijing agreed, as stated in the Basic Law, to consider holding universal suffrage "in the light of the actual situation" and "in accordance with the principle of gradual and orderly progress". It further states that "the ultimate aims are the selection of the Chief Executive by universal suffrage upon nomination by a broadly representative nominating committee in accordance with democratic procedures and the election of all the members of the Legislative Council by universal suffrage".

The pan-democratic camp, however, strongly objected to the screening of the candidates by the nominating committee. The radicals called for its abolition and asked for "genuine direct election", while the moderates suggested that the committee should accept and nominate candidates proposed by the public and political parties. The civic and political party nominations, in the view of legal experts, were not consistent with the stipulations in the Basic Law. In Beijing's view, the requirement of screening candidates by the nominating committee to ensure that the selected candidates "love (loyal to) the country and love Hong Kong" was a necessary prerequisite. Beijing would not allow a free-for-all situation in which an uncooperative or even a confrontational candidate could be selected and voted in as Chief Executive. The views of the pan-democrats were very much different from those of the pro-Beijing politicians and the government. The government submitted a constitutional reform bill which stipulated that all candidates for Chief Executive Election had to be screened and approved by the Nominating Committee, and universal suffrage could be adopted in Chief Executive Election. Unfortunately, the reform bill was rejected by the Legislative Council. As a result, there was no universal suffrage for the Chief Executive Election in 2017. The new Chief Executive Mrs Carrie Lam was elected by the Election Committee consisting of 1,200 members. This was a step backward, resulting in no progress towards universal suffrage and greater democratisation in Hong Kong.

3. *"One Country, Two Systems" (OCTS)*

Developments during the two decades since the handover of Hong Kong have not all been smooth and satisfactory. Many unsettled issues such as universal suffrage and inadequate public housing have led to protests and divisiveness, which hinder effective governance by the Hong Kong government.

The protests can be attributed to political, social and age differences. First, Hong Kong residents had lived under the British colonial rule and were accustomed to free speech and non-governmental intervention. Some of the older generation fled to Hong Kong from the mainland in 1949 and are suspicious of any moves by China. Younger people who are educated in Western curricula and culture tend to be supporters of the democratic camp. Besides, there is a large expatriate community consisting of retired civil servants and Western journalists who are not friendly towards the Hong Kong government and Beijing. Although vocal challengers are the minority, they call the tune while the majority remain silent as they just want to keep a stable job and live peacefully. Second, businessmen and entrepreneurs have benefited from economic growth during the last two decades. They largely support the establishment and the central government. Working class people, on the other hand, encounter problems like rising costs of living and inadequate affordable housing. They have become agitated and are against the government and establishment. Third, young people — including students, school leavers, undergraduates, fresh graduates and young employees — are mostly idealistic and impatient with slow changes in social conditions and their personal well-being. Mature people who are more aware of their family obligation and social responsibility are more realistic and they support a stable social and political setting. These people, young and old, fall into two large groups — the pro-democracy and pro-establishment group. The Pan-Democratic camp has been confrontational and against the local and central government in many instances. The pro-establishment camp supports Beijing and Hong Kong government in general except for certain unpopular government policies. The divide has hampered legislative process and policy implementation. It has also affected Beijing's confidence and trust in Hong Kong. Beijing has warned Hong Kong that "Hong Kong would lose everything should the OCTS fail". It further reminds Hong Kong that the high degree of autonomy is a delegation of power by the central government, not power sharing between the two. It cannot be used to confront Beijing.

As the central government is quite annoyed by anti-Beijing protests in Hong Kong, will the OCTS be scrapped before its maturity in 2047? Given the current situation, Beijing is likely to be more assertive and the OCTS can be more restrictive if defiance against Beijing continues. The OCTS will evolve along a bumpy path. It is, however, unlikely that the OCTS will be suspended because Beijing is keen to demonstrate that the OCTS can succeed in Hong Kong.

4. *Inadequate affordable housing*

One of the major factors causing unhappiness among Hong Kong residents, particularly young people, is the lack of affordable housing. Hong Kong property prices have been rising, albeit with temporary declines at times, such that buying a house is an unrealisable dream for many people. The reasons are, first, inadequate land supply for housing; second, influx of foreign buyers especially from the mainland; and third, lack of public housing.

Public housing is an important factor which can enhance social stability for a city or country. Apart from providing a shelter for residents at reasonably low costs, it serves as a means to enable residents to share economic growth through capital gains in properties. In Singapore, more than 80 percent of Singapore residents live in public housing known as Housing Development Board (HDB) flats and most of them are flat owners, and it has contributed significantly to social and political stability there. Although nearly 50 percent of Hong Kong residents live in flats built by governmental housing authorities, the public housing scheme has not been as successful as Singapore. Many problems exist and it has become a political issue. In Hong Kong, most public flat dwellers are tenants, and only a very low percentage are owners. Even for those flats sold to residents, one of the problems is that many units of flats under the Subsidised Home Ownership Scheme have been left vacant. The reason is that when the flats were sold earlier, the price did not include the land cost. When flat owners wish to sell their flats after a stipulated period of, say, 5 years, they have to buy the apportioned lands at the prevailing market price. As land prices have rocketed to such a high level in recent years, the amounts which they have to pay for lands are so substantial that they find it not worthwhile to sell their flats, unless the location is exceptionally good and they could get a high price for their flats. The system of selling the flat excluding land cost deprives the owner of a share of capital gains as the economy grows. Moreover, the flat could become too small as the family expands, and eventually be left unoccupied after the family moves to a bigger flat bought in the private market. As such, it is a waste of resources in keeping the flat vacant and unoccupied. The Housing Authority, representing the government, cannot recover the money for the land cost which is embedded in the flat. The government, the flat owner and society are all losers as the flat cannot be released for better use by someone who really needs it. The solution is to sell all flats under the Home Ownership Scheme inclusive of the land cost. The purchaser can then sell his flat in the market after the stipulated period of occupation or rent it out freely in the rental market. For the existing flats sold earlier, the owners should only be required to reimburse the original land cost at the time of purchase plus interest. All will gain as the flat owner can obtain capital gains for his property, and the government can recover the land cost hidden in the flat.

The second problem is the high percentage of public flats available for renting and that their rents are overly low. The ultimate objective of public housing is to enable more residents to purchase their own properties, not renting them. Although the "Tenant Purchase Scheme" was designed to encourage tenants to rent first and purchase later, it has not been effective as the rents are too low that there is no incentive for the tenants to purchase the flats. It is costly for the government to hold on to too many rental flats as the rents received can never cover the ever-increasing maintenance costs. And it is almost impossible to raise rents as any rental increase proposals will be met with unhappiness and protests, which could also cost votes in the elections. The consequence is to subsidise the tenants continuously without an ending date. Some tenants have become richer now and moved into their private flats, but they still retain their public flats for storage or keep them vacant for other purposes. It is untenable and unsustainable to keep subsidising tenants without limits by maintaining a large number of rental flats. The solution is to sell the existing rental flats inclusive of land cost to the sitting tenants, and confine the supply of new rental flats to the needy with a termination clause in the tenancy agreement.

Singapore

Unlike Hong Kong, Singapore does not have the above political and constitutional problems. Under the Westminster system, Singapore voters use the one-man-one-vote system to elect their members of parliament (MPs). The political party which has won a majority of seats in Parliament forms the government. MPs elect a leader to become Prime Minister, who appoints some MPs to be Ministers and heads the Cabinet. On housing, more than 80 percent of Singapore residents own and reside in low cost flats provided by the Housing & Development Board (HDB). Public housing has been affordable and successful in Singapore. Despite the success in providing Singaporeans stable jobs and affordable housing, Singapore may face several challenges in the years ahead.

1. *Welfarism trap*

The saying that "there is no free lunch and everyone should work and earn his or her own living" is well-known in Singapore. The Singapore government has rejected the idea of welfarism since gaining its independence in 1965.

After a few decades of development, the economy has grown substantially, but the distribution of the fruits of growth has not been even, which is to be expected in a competitive meritocracy where greater rewards go to those who succeed.

Income disparity hence becomes greater, and the divide between the successful and the poor becomes more evident. The government has mitigated inequality by providing affordable housing and public transport, better healthcare and the Workfare supplement to help low-wage workers.

After the General Election in 2011, the government dished out more goodies to help the low- and middle-income groups. HDB grants, healthcare benefits, baby bonuses and other subsidies have increased. This gives an impression that the Singapore government has started moving towards welfarism.

People's desire for a change of lifestyle and an increase in living standards will force the government to increase the types and amounts of transfers over the years. This is particularly true in a democratic regime where the electorate can use votes to make demands. The government will have to either increase marginal tax rates, making income taxes and property taxes more progressive, and/or levy new taxes to finance the ever increasing transfers and freebies.

The government should be mindful to avoid falling into the welfarism trap as voters' demands may be insatiable and transfers can, over the years, snowball into unbearable burdens. The government should, therefore, dampen the request for more transfers and prevent Singapore from becoming a welfare state, similar to those in the West.

2. *Regional security and terrorist threats*

Singapore's strategic location is a natural asset for the nation. It also becomes a point of rivalry between big powers due to its strategic value. United States, China and Japan have exerted their influence in the South China Sea in which Vietnam, the Philippines and China are embroiled in disputes of territorial claims. Singapore's call for action to ensure freedom of navigation in the area was mistakenly interpreted as taking sides in the disputes. The claims and counterclaims have threatened regional stability, which may affect navigation freedom and Singapore's security if the disputes escalate and the situation deteriorates further.

International terrorist threats pose another challenge for Singapore. The defeat of ISIS in Iraq and Syria may result in it moving its bases to Indonesia, and southern parts of Thailand and the Philippines where the populations are predominantly Muslim. Islam radicalism can take root and grow in Southeast Asia, and major cities, including Singapore, could be hit by terrorist attacks similar to those in London and Paris.

3. *Small nation diplomacy*

Singapore has been reminded repeatedly that it is small, a small red dot on the map of the world. Being a small country, Singapore has to walk precariously between bigger countries in the neighbourhood, as well as big powers in the world. The United States replaced European colonial rulers in the region in the early part of the 20th century, and has exerted its strong influence in Asia since the ending of the Second World War, the Korean War and the Vietnam War. The Chinese economy, on the other hand, has emerged as the second largest in the world after continued high growth in the last few decades. China is now more assertive in regional affairs, and is poised to become a challenger to American leadership in Asia.

How should Singapore behave as a small nation amid the competition of big powers? Professor Kishore Mahbubani, Former Dean of Lee Kuan

Yew School of Public Policy, National University of Singapore, drew a lesson from the sanctions of Qatar by bigger Arab nations and concluded that small states must be realistic and must behave like small states. This has prompted a rebuttal from Ambassador Bilahari Kausikan who stated that "Of course we recognise asymmetries of size and power. But that does not mean we must grovel or accept subordination as a norm of relationship." This shows that even two brilliant minds in diplomacy cannot agree with each other on the correct manner and way for Singapore to deal with big powers. It is therefore necessary to tread carefully in handling diplomatic relationships with bigger countries in the region and big world powers in order to safeguard Singapore's interests.

Conclusion

Hong Kong and Singapore share a common background of being former British colonies. Their legal systems and judiciaries are similar, and the rule of law constitutes an important pillar in both societies. Economic structures in both places are also similar in that the service sector contributes 70 percent of GDP. The sizes of their economies are about the same, roughly around US$300 billion in recent years.

The differences between them are that Hong Kong is now part of China, and Singapore is an independent nation. The Chinese central government is responsible for Hong Kong's defence and foreign affairs, while Singapore has to build its military forces for defence and handle its own diplomatic affairs. While Singapore has Westminster-style parliamentary democracy, Hong Kong's political system is unique and is still evolving under the OCTS framework.

The challenges faced by Hong Kong and Singapore are also different. In Hong Kong, the evolution of its political system and socioeconomic as well as political divides are difficult problems without easy solutions. In Singapore, strong political leadership is needed to ensure sustained economic growth, more equitable distribution of wealth as well as minimize security and terrorism threats. It is also necessary to raise Singapore's profile in the international arena albeit its status as a small country. However, strong leadership and democracy move in different directions, for instance, full democracy in Taiwan has weakened political leadership there. Young people in Singapore receive Western-style education and are influenced by Western culture and they tend to be more liberal and less accepting of the notion of strong leadership. After the pioneer generation is gone and a few younger generations have emerged, it may be difficult to convince them of the need for strong political leadership. Singapore will have to find new ways to sustain economic growth and create an inclusive society, internally, and strengthen its defence capability and practise its "small nation but impactful diplomacy" externally. These are likely achievable if the people are united with a common objective in striving for a better future for Singapore.

Shenzhen–Hong Kong:

Review and Outlook*

GUO Wanda

Dr. GUO Wanda is Executive Vice President of China Development Institute (CDI) and Vice Chairman of Chinese Association of Hong Kong & Macao Studies.

He specializes in macroeconomics, industrial policy, urbanization, low-carbon economy, Hong Kong & Macao and Guangdong–Hong Kong–Macao Cooperation. He played leading roles in more than 100 research projects commissioned by Chinese central and local governments and published books like *Rethinking China's Urbanization and Metropolis, Migrant Workers' Early Retirement: Theory, Evidence and Policy, Low Carbon City: A Non-Regret Opinion*, and *Perspective on the Development between Shenzhen & Hong Kong and the integration of the PRD Region*, etc. He was awarded the Chevening Fellowship by the British government in 2008.

He received his Ph.D. in economics from Nankai University in 1991.

In 1968, when Mr. Lee Kuan Yew referred to Hong Kong and Singapore as twin cities, many people in Shenzhen illegally escaped to Hong Kong due to the extreme difference in terms of wealth between the two places.

---

* This is a translated version of the original speech in Mandarin.

This significant event impelled the opening-up policy proposed by Mr. Deng Xiaoping. Shenzhen became the frontier of the opening-up policy, bearing the mission to test how the socialist mainland China can learn from the capitalist Hong Kong.

Shenzhen initially welcomed a lot of Hong Kong factories, forming the "store in front, factory in back" economic pattern. Without which, there will not be the prosperous Shenzhen today. Since 2000, processing trade in Shenzhen has declined from 70% to the current 30%, which means the transferring of manufacturing and processing trade from Hong Kong to Shenzhen has decreased. This is partially a result of the booming population that originally migrated to Shenzhen due to the huge demand for labour in processing trade. If it was twenty years ago, they might have escaped to Hong Kong, but now these people are staying in Shenzhen, and fostering Shenzhen's high-tech industry which is independent from Hong Kong economy, privately owned, and self-motivated. Given the ever-growing population of adventurers and opening-up policy, the high-tech industry took off.

The relocation of the processing industry to Shenzhen is the main reason for the expansion of service industry in Hong Kong, which accounts for nearly 98% of Hong Kong industry by present. On the other hand, due to the rising of manufacturing, processing and high-tech industries, Shenzhen is in need of service industry as well. In early stages, service industries, such as the financial industry, developed independently from Hong Kong, but gradually became impossible as they matured. So, if we look closely, because of Hong Kong, Shenzhen was able to transform from a fishing village that escaped to Hong Kong into a metropolis just like Hong Kong.

Shenzhen started as a small village, but has experienced dramatic changes in the last three decades, especially the last one. GDP of Hong Kong increased by 1.8 times, while the change of Shenzhen was much more dramatic, increasing by 18 times. Shenzhen's GDP has increased from 10% to 100% of Hong Kong's GDP. Nonetheless, GDP per capita of Shenzhen is half of the statistics of Hong Kong.

An important factor of influence is population. The current population of Shenzhen is 12 million, almost the combined population of Hong Kong and Singapore. The actual population of Shenzhen is 20 million and

I estimate that it will continue to grow. Shenzhen has greatly benefited from the demographic dividend, as seen in the population and economic development. For example, Shenzhen airport's passenger flow is over 40 million. Just yesterday, I took a direct flight from Shenzhen to Singapore which was impossible before. Now, there are a lot of international flights to Tokyo, Seoul and even Los Angeles. Similarly, Shenzhen port saw fast development as well — the harbours of Shenzhen and Hong Kong combined will be the largest port in the world. Housing price in Shenzhen is soaring up and almost catching up with that of Hong Kong, after learning from its teacher, Hong Kong, of how to make revenue from auctioning off recovered land.

There is a big difference between Hong Kong and Shenzhen in terms of research and development. The private enterprises and organizations in Shenzhen put a lot of effort into research, taking up 4.1% of the population, while in Hong Kong it is mostly government initiated and is only 0.8% of the GDP. In my opinion, this major difference between Shenzhen and Hong Kong lies in their research and development in the past two decades. If we look back carefully, we will find that the rise of Alibaba, Tencent and Huawei took place in the past twenty years. While Hong Kong has been a bit out of step with this latest wave of high-tech development, Shenzhen has drawn power from it and moved a long way with a very quick pace.

Hong Kong still plays an important role in the development of Shenzhen and has a close relationship with Shenzhen in the respects of industry development, urban development and institutional evolution. Taking a view from the other way around, we should consider whether the rise of Shenzhen will benefit Hong Kong or not, especially for the service industry. It is important for us to review the advantages to Hong Kong. During a speech in Europe, I was asked to talk about competition between Hong Kong and Shanghai. While I refused their suggestion, I told them instead, that I must talk about the *cooperation* between Hong Kong and Shenzhen. Undeniably there is competition between Hong Kong and the mainland, but the cooperation is much more important.

Having looked at the rise of Hong Kong and Shenzhen, let us turn to the next ten or twenty years. Just as Mr. Leung referred in previous speech, President Xi Jinping witnessed the signing of the *Framework*

Agreement on Deepening Guangdong–Hong Kong–Macao Cooperation in the Development of the Bay Area on 1 July 2017. China Development Institute, the research institute that I work for, is located in Shenzhen. We proposed that Hong Kong should have a larger hinterland for building a closer connection with the mainland. We think one important reason for such a lot of problems faced by Hong Kong now, such as industry, people's wellbeing, as well as housing mentioned by Professor Ker Sin Tze just now, are due to the limited land space of Hong Kong. While its neighbour Shenzhen has a land twice as big as Hong Kong, plus Dongguan and other places, Greater Bay area can provide vast hinterland for Hong Kong.

In a metropolitan area, administrative divisions are broken, allowing free flow of all production factors. A hot topic explores innovation of "One Country, Two Systems". Besides custom clearance, other issues, such as inspection and quarantine, people and finance mobility, can be approached with special arrangement like the Shenzhen–Hong Kong Stock Connect programme. The essence is to benefit from operating as "one country", at the same time taking advantage of "two systems".

Generally speaking, Hong Kong and Macau will certainly play an important role in the development of the Greater Bay Area. These two cities must be vital centres in China Pearl River Delta and exert radiational effect in that area. Before I came to Singapore yesterday, I was in Hezhou, Guangxi Province, a city within two hours of travel by high-speed rail from Shenzhen. Hezhou government officials hoped that Hezhou can be a backyard for Hong Kong and Greater Bay area. I think this is a reasonable expectation considering the three-hour travel time between Hezhou and Hong Kong — two-hour railway from Hezhou to Shenzhen, and one-hour subway from Shenzhen to Hong Kong.

Therefore, the Greater Bay area should provide infrastructure connection. When I visited San Francisco Bay Area, I rented a car to drive to Berkeley and was stuck in terrifying jam on the bridge, which inspired me to consider just how many bridges are enough for the Greater Bay area. From my hindsight view, I think the Hong Kong–Zhuhai–Macao Bridge is essential and necessary indeed. The population of Greater Bay area will be much larger than that of San Francisco Bay Area and we suppose that the economy in the area will be very active. So, the Greater Bay area should put a lot of efforts in infrastructural connections, such as high-speed rail, ports and tunnels, as its status is far from enough at present.

Last year, after years of elaborations, Hong Kong and Shenzhen had agreed to jointly develop an innovation and technology park in Lok Ma Chau Loop. Development of the park is led by a Hong Kong tech park company, within whose board of directors Shenzhen side only holds three seats. At present, Shenzhen is moving faster than Hong Kong. An area of three square kilometre, and possibly expanded to five square kilometres, the Shenzhen side is designated for high tech and innovation, with the Southern University of Science and Technology campus already set up. The Hong Kong side has set up an innovation centre, which is subordinate to the Hong Kong Productivity Council, in the Hong Kong–Shenzhen Innovation and Technology Park. Qianhai and Shekou Free Trade Zone, which is led by Shenzhen, is also designated for bilateral cooperation with Hong Kong.

It is a pity that the action on the Hong Kong side is relatively slower compared with Shenzhen. The development potential is quite large and success depends on how it is carried out. As for Qianhai and Shekou Free Trade Zone, which Shenzhen has taken lead on, there is still huge potential for Hong Kong to explore. In the future, "One Country, Two Systems" will exert its advantages in making Shenzhen and the Greater Bay area a vast hinterland for Hong Kong. The universities in Hong Kong will be able to collaborate with the manufacturing industries in Shenzhen and Dongguan, forming the Shenzhen–Hong Kong Metropolis.

Another issue is living arrangements and to ease Hong Kong residents' settlement in Shenzhen in terms of employment, education, investment, as well as housing. Hong Kong residents' "equal treatment" in the mainland is part of the planning of the Greater Bay.

深港"双城记":
回顾与展望

郭万达

请允许我用中文来演讲。很高兴来参加这个论坛,大家一个上午都讲香港和新加坡,主办方让我来讲深圳,好像有点第三者插足的感觉。

为什么要讲深圳和香港的关系呢? 在 1968 年,李光耀先生讲香港和新加坡是双城的时候,深圳那时候还在 "逃港",大家都知道"逃港" 是什么意思吧? 就是很多深圳人都偷渡逃到香港,因为香港很富,深圳很穷。"逃港" 事件是促使邓小平先生实行开放政策的一个重要因素,办法就是设立深圳经济特区来进行改革开放的试验。邓小平在深圳画了一个圈,说我来看一看社会主义的中国能不能跟资本主义的香港学一些东西,来看看能不能也像香港那样发展。

那么之后发生了什么故事呢? 一开始深圳就是承接了香港的很多工厂,很多的工厂到了深圳,那么这就是香港和深圳之间的 "前店后厂"。深圳如果没有香港当时的加工业的转移,深圳的制造业就发展不到今天的水平。但是,1992 年之后,特别是 2000 年以后,深圳的加工贸易是持续下降的,90 年代的时候加工贸易占了百分之七十以上,到今天占到百分之三十。这说明什么呢? 说明香港的加工业转移的模式在深圳的角色和地位下降了。是什么支撑了深圳的发展呢? 2000 年以后,深圳独立发展了高科技产业,这些高科技产业并不是从香港延伸出来的,深圳的高科技企业都是民营的,是相对独立地崛起出来的,这一点非常重要。

深圳因为有了制造业, 有了高科技, 深圳也要发展服务业。刚开始深圳的服务业也是受香港的影响, 但后来深圳的服务业发展也很快, 比如金融, 深圳已经是一个重要的金融中心。因为香港, 深圳从一个 "逃港" 的小渔村, 发展成为一个跟香港比肩的现代化大都市。

深圳和香港之间的变化主要是在1997年之后的这二十年, 特别是最近十年, 深圳发生了很大的变化。香港在过去二十年间, GDP (国内生产总值) 总量增长了1.8倍, 这已经是不错了, 但是这和深圳相比仍有差距, 深圳在20年间的GDP总量已增长了18倍多。二十年前, 深圳的GDP总量只及香港的10%, 现在已经接近香港。当然, 论人均的GDP, 深圳和香港比还是有差距, 深圳只及香港的一半左右。

另外很重要的是人口的变化, 现在虽然深圳的常住人口是一千二百万, 几乎是香港加新加坡的人口。但实际上深圳的人口不是一千多万, 已经是两千多万人口的超大城市, 我估计深圳的人口还是控制不住。人口迁移给深圳带来的红利是非常明显的。人口和经济的增长, 带给深圳很多的变化, 比如机场, 深圳的客流量已经超过4000万人次。以前深圳没有国际航班, 现在深圳已经开通了很多的国际航班, 昨天我是直接从深圳飞到新加坡, 深圳还开通了到东京、到首尔、到洛杉矶的国际航班了。深圳港口发展也很快, 如果我们把深圳和香港加在一起, 那就是全球最大的集装箱港了。当然房价也涨了很多, 深圳也跟香港靠齐, 深圳拍卖土地是学香港, 香港就是老师, 香港教会我们怎么去把土地收来然后再拍卖, 卖地成为政府的一个收入, 所以房价也是往香港那边靠齐。

有一个巨大的区别, 就是香港的研发比较少, 只占 GDP 的0.8%, 但深圳在研发投入比较多, 占 GDP 的 4.1%, 而且主要是来自民营企业和私人机构的研发投资。香港的研发投入主要还是政府的。我认为二十年里, 这是深圳和香港的重大的区别。仔细想想, 这二十年就是腾讯崛起的二十年, 就是华为崛起的二十年, 就是比亚迪崛起的二十年, 深圳抓住了互联网的机会, 发展了高科技。但香港这二十年却是错过了这个机会, 这是深圳和香港的一个区别。

总结一下, 从回顾来看, 香港的因素对深圳来讲是非常重要的, 无论是产业发展、城市发展、体制的演进都跟香港有密切的关系。当然反过来看, 深圳的崛起是不是也支持了香港的发展? 有一次我在欧洲参加一个论坛, 给我出的演讲的题目是让我讲香港和上海怎么竞争, 我说 "不行", 我一定要讲香港和深圳怎么合作。因为我认为, 若问香港与内地的竞争有没有, 肯定有, 但合作更加重要, 通过合作, 你影响我, 我也影响你。

　　那么，未来的十年、二十年，深圳和香港又会怎么发展呢？是一种什么样的关系呢？刚才梁锦松先生演讲时提到，国家已经启动了粤港澳大湾区建设的框架合作协议，这个大湾区既包括了香港、澳门，也包括了广东 9 个重要城市，包括深圳、广州。我的看法，这是香港的一个很重要的机会，因为香港要更大的腹地，使得香港和内地的联系会更紧密起来。香港在过去的二十年，为什么在产业上、在民生上有问题，就是它的空间非常的有限，没有发展的空间。深圳的面面积是香港一倍，地方比香港大很多，如果再加上大湾区的其他周边城市，如东莞、惠州等，对香港来讲就有了一个更大的腹地，更大的市场。

　　粤港澳大湾区就是一个大都市圈（metropolitan area），这就要打破行政阻隔，主要还有跨境的阻隔，使生产要素能够自由地流动，发挥"一国两制"的优势，"两制"不能成为要素流动的障碍。那么，怎么样在"两制"这个问题上要有所创新呢？比如，能不能在大湾区下，包括通关的问题，涉及人流、物流、资金流，有没有特殊的（比如像深港通）一些制度安排。这是目前正在讨论的一个问题，就是怎么样发挥"一国"这个便利，然后把"两制"这个优势发挥出来，这个是非常重要的。

　　总而言之，香港、澳门一定是粤港澳大湾区中的一个很重要的中心城市，然后在珠江三角洲往外辐射，把这个腹地范围影响到泛珠三角。前几天我到广西的贺州市，从深圳到贺州坐高铁就两个小时。贺州的领导对我说，贺州要成为粤港澳大湾区的后花园。我说从香港到贺州也就三个小时，你也可以成为香港的后花园。

　　因此，这个粤港澳大湾区首先要提供基础设施的互联互通。上个月我到旧金山湾区，我去了斯坦福，也去了伯克利，我自己租了辆车在旧金山湾区走，也过了几个桥，感觉就是堵车，堵车，堵车。所以这给我一个启发，将来在这个粤港澳大湾区有多少桥是合适的。基础设施的联通，不仅是跨江的大桥，还要有跨江的轻轨，否则靠汽车，就容易堵车。

　　在这个大湾区下，香港和深圳之间的联系会越来越多。深圳和香港已经签订了关于河套的合作开发，一平方公里的河套是香港来主导开发，发展创新科技；深圳这边有一个三平方公里（可能会扩大到五平方公里），由深圳来主导开发，形成"1+3"的模式。当然，刚才提到的还有深圳前海蛇口的自贸园区，这个也是深圳为主导的，但其实仍然是为了和香港合作。也就是说，深圳和香港合作，就

是要利用 "一国两制" 的优势, 使得深圳和大湾区能够成为香港的一个腹地, 促进香港的大学的研发能够和深圳、东莞的制造业结合起来, 深港共同形成一个大都会区。

香港居民到内地如何更方便地就业, 如何更方便生活？现在我们叫 "同等待遇", 就是怎么样使香港的居民到内地, 特别是在深圳能够更方便地生活、投资和就业, 而解决这些问题的政策已经在规划之中。

Singapore and Hong Kong Should Firmly Grasp New Development Opportunities in China*

LIANG Hai Ming

Professor LIANG Hai Ming, Chairman and Chief Economist of China Silk Road iValley Research Institute, Expert representative in Belt and Road Forum for International Cooperation, Senior Fellow, Institute of Advanced Studies, Nanyang Technological University, Singapore and Financial Commentator of China Central Television.

He mainly focuses on the area of the Belt and Road, free trade zone, co-operation between Guangdong, Hong Kong and Macau, macroeconomics and cross-cultural communications.

Today, besides the problems or challenges faced by Singapore and Hong Kong, I would like to discuss the cooperation space between the two cities in the future. I think Singapore and Hong Kong should cooperate in the following two respects.

---

* This is a translated version of the original speech in Mandarin.

Firstly, Singapore and Hong Kong should cooperate in setting up an Innovative Enterprise Exchange. Owing to my frequent travels between Hong Kong, Singapore and China, my observation is that when an enterprise, especially a Chinese enterprise, is preparing to do Initial Public Offering (IPO), all the exchanges in Hong Kong, Shenzhen, Shanghai, as well as Singapore will compete for this deal. Based on this situation, we should consider cooperating and doing some innovative enterprises rather than striving for traditional business. Currently, there are quite a lot of innovative enterprises in China and even the whole world.

The growth rate of China's start-ups has been nearly 100% per year since 2010, ranking first in the world. The growth rate is almost twice that of the United Kingdom, which ranks second in the world. Under these circumstances, lots of Chinese start-ups hope to be listed on overseas stock markets. However, they often meet various problems, such as "same stock with different rights", as well as some technical issues. Under such conditions, a lot of enterprises will choose foreign countries, especially the United States (US), for IPO, rather than the exchanges of Shenzhen and Shanghai. That is no different from letting money and opportunities go over to other countries. Then how can these problems be resolved? It can be realised by setting up an exchange that is jointly run by Singapore and Hong Kong as a collaborative venture. The joint venture exchange may be located either in Singapore or Hong Kong and managed or operated by both parties. The joint venture may consider being innovative in terms of rules, systems and techniques by adopting or combining US, European Union or Australian exchange rules. Naturally, this is only possible with the reality of Singapore and Hong Kong's market conditions acting as the basis of consideration. The exchange may also use the RMB as the currency of transaction and settlement in place of the US dollar and Hong Kong dollar.

The main purpose of setting up this exchange is for the purpose of attracting both Chinese innovative enterprises which are considering listing in the US and those already listed in the US, but still wishing to list in other exchanges. The joint venture exchange operated by Singapore and Hong Kong will cater for such demands.

The Innovative Enterprise Exchange will cover a wide scope, including innovative enterprises in China, Singapore, Hong Kong, Southeast

Asian countries, Asian countries, as well as countries along the "Belt and Road". The significance of this innovative enterprise exchange rests in the following three areas. First, innovative enterprises which wish to list on the exchange will bring huge business opportunities for Singapore and Hong Kong. Second, the new exchange with RMB as the currency of transaction and settlement, will further promote Singapore and Hong Kong as offshore RMB centres. Third, the innovative enterprise exchange can act as a safe haven for international financial markets. After the global financial crisis in 2008, international markets have been uncertain about the US dollar (as anchor currency) as well as the dollar's dominance of international finance. The world hopes to decrease dependence on the US dollar as settlement currency and the accompanying risks of exchange rate fluctuation, credit and devaluation risk, as well as the risk of contagion from future US financial crises which could endanger other countries' economic and financial systems.

Beside the innovative enterprise exchange, we can consider jointly setting up an exit strategy platform for innovative enterprises in the future. Innovation potentially creates a new economy; therefore, it is an important path to consider if we are to realise sustainable and healthy development of economy and society. However, looking around the world, whether it is science and technology innovation or start-ups, there are more examples of failure than success, especially start-ups which engage in advanced and disruptive innovation. These tend to suffer a wide range of problems more easily. As entrepreneurial business experience around the world demonstrates, the chance of success for an entrepreneur who has previously failed is much higher than that of a first-time entrepreneur. Only with stronger support for those who may have failed in innovation and enterprise, whose failure was not due to moral hazards, will the success rate in innovation and enterprise be higher. An innovative idea or product may be temporarily considered a "failure" in China, but that does not mean that it will be branded a "failure" by the whole world.

Even if an innovative idea or product of a Chinese enterprise cannot be accepted in the domestic market of China, with the help of Singapore and Hong Kong's international resources and connections, it can still be marketed and sold to countries along the "Belt and Road" or even the entire world. This could well-resuscitate some entrepreneurs and innovative products. Singapore and Hong Kong should cooperate in setting up an exit strategy platform for innovative enterprise and jointly seek and nurture Chinese businesses with huge potential, such as Alibaba and Tencent, which will bring enormous economic benefits for Singapore and Hong Kong. A well-known example is Tencent. In the late 90s, Tencent faced collapse and its founder announced to the market that he will sell this company for 1 million US dollars. At that time, neither US companies nor Japanese companies would like to invest in it, as they were all uncertain about the future of this innovative Chinese enterprise and believed that they would not be able to recoup their investment. In the end, a South Africa company invested in Tencent, as 1 million US dollars was not a big amount for this company. Now, Tencent has been listed and that South Africa company has recouped its investment with a 4000-fold return.

Another example is Alibaba, a better-known case. In its start-up phase, Jack Ma thought Alibaba was going to collapse and tried to introduce investment. Our Singaporean friends did not invest in Alibaba at that time, but the Japanese did. The Japanese have recouped their investment in Alibaba with more than 1000-fold return by now. What we can learn from this case is that there are lots of innovative Chinese enterprises with potential, but it is not easy for us to foresee the future potential of these enterprises. Under these circumstances, Singapore and Hong Kong, armed with international perspectives and mindsets, should consider investing in these innovative enterprises, especially temporarily unsustainable enterprises.

In conclusion, China is developing with great speed and there is a rapid rise in its middle and high-income classes. As a survey has shown, those with over RMB 10 million in investable assets in China stands at approximately 1.58 million. This figure, compared with that of 180,000 in 2006, shows a nine-fold increase. This is the equivalent of nearly 400 people becoming multimillionaires per day. Therefore, there is a huge demand among such groups for asset allocation and management services. Furthermore, there are two hundred million middle-class citizens. The figure is set to grow in the future, which means middle-class consumer demand will continue to grow. Based on such a situation, I think Singapore and Hong Kong should pay attention to the business opportunities offered by the hundreds of millions of middle-class citizens in China.

Statistics show that, despite the waning of the "population bonus" in the manufacturing industry in China, the "population bonus" of finance, services and consumption is just getting off the ground. In terms of the figures involved, there is no other country in the world which has such a huge and definitive business opportunity as China. It is more important than ever for Singapore and Hong Kong to pay close attention to the development opportunities in China and firmly grasp the newly-emerging population bonus in China.

新加坡与香港应该紧握中国
发展新机遇

梁海明

今天我想给大家带来的是新加坡和香港未来是否有合作的空间，而不只是大家看到的问题或挑战。我认为香港和新加坡未来可以在以下两个方面进行合作。

第一个方面就是设立一个创新企业交易所。过去，因为我经常往返香港和新加坡还有中国大陆，我经常看到一家企业，尤其是一家中国企业准备上市 Initial Public Offering（IPO）的时候，不仅是港交所在抢，深交所、上交所在抢，新加坡的交易所也在抢这个交易。所以在这种情况下，是否未来可以不要去抢那种传统的产业，而是大家去合作，去做一些创新的产业？目前不仅仅是全球各国的创新的企业数量非常多，中国的创新企业的数量也是非常多的。

自 2010 年以来，每年中国的创新企业是以 100 巴仙的速度增长的，排在世界第一位——它的速度比排在第二位的英国高出了两倍。在这种情况下，很多中国的创新企业都希望可以到海外去上市。但是，过程中又遇到了各种各样的问题，包括"同股不同权"，还有一些技术的因素。在这种情况下，很多的企业最终就不能留在深交所、上交所，就去了外国，尤其是美国，去那里上市。这样就等于是肥水流了他人田了。那怎么去解决呢？可否由新加坡和香港设立一个创新企业的交易所，大家共同出资，共同管理？这个交易所的地点可以是新加坡，也可以是香港，这个可以谈。而这个交易所上市的规则、制度和技术在设置上可以进行一些创新。在考虑新交所和港交所目前的这种规则之下，可以结合采用美国、澳

69

大利亚或欧洲交易所的原则。而且这些交易所可以考虑以人民币作为交易和结算的货币。

但我们设立这个交易所的时候，最主要的目的一方面是为了吸引这些中国的创新企业的上市，另一方面就是吸引在美国的企业，尤其是在美国上市的一些企业。这是因为很多在美国的创新企业，包括中国的，也希望去别的交易所上市，而这个交易所正好适合他们过来。

范围可以很广，例如中国、香港、新加坡、东南亚国家、亚洲国家，甚至是一带一路沿线国家的创新企业都可以上市。它的意义在哪里呢？首先，有企业过来这里进行 IPO，肯定是会为这个城市、这个交易所带来庞大的商机。第二，就是可以使用人民币作为这个交易和结算货币。在这种情况下，确实是可以推动新加坡和香港进一步发展成人民币的离岸中心。另外，设立的这个创新企业交易所，可以成为国际金融市场的避风港，因为每次发生环球金融危机或者是亚洲金融危机时，都会受到冲击。如果能有个交易所，它将减少以美元或英镑或日元交易，而是以人民币交易。它或许可以成为一个避风港，受到的冲击不会这么大。

另外，除了这个合作交易所之外，未来可能也可以共建一个创新企业退场机制的平台因为我发现现在很多创新企业，不管是中国还是在欧美国家创新企业的失败率都比较高。但是，如果失败之后，这些创新企业能够重新创业，它们的成功率又会非常高——成功率可以达到百分之六十。在这种情况下，失败了不是真正的失败，尤其是第一次失败不能算是真正的失败。所以，这些失败的理念或产品即使在中国被视作为失败了，在全球的范围内却未必是失败的，而且是不被接受和认定的一种失败。

在这种情况下，新加坡和香港完全可以通过自己的国际资源和人脉，向全世界各国，尤其是一带一路沿线国家推广、出售在中国内地被称为失败的一些企业，或者是一些点子。或许这可以令这些创业者和新产品起死回生。而且，新加坡和香港共建这个企业退场机制，共同去寻找、培育像阿里巴巴、腾讯这种有庞大潜力的中国企业，是可以给新加坡和香港带来非常大的经济效益的。我举个大家可能都知道的例子，在上个世纪九十年代，腾讯基本上是办不下去了。所以腾讯的创始人就在市场公布说，谁给我一百万美元，我这家公司给他。当时欧美企业、日本企业都不大愿意去投资，不知道这个创新企业未来有没有前途，觉得如果投资 100 万美元，公司却失败了，不就是赔了吗？最后是南非的一家公司觉得一百万对它来说不多，便决定去投资。现在，腾讯上市了，南非的投资得到了四千倍的回报。这是腾讯的例子。

阿里巴巴，可能大家更加清楚这个例子。就是当时马云也准备干不下去了，所以就引进很多的投资。咱们新加坡没有投资（我说的是以前），但是日本的网民去投资了这个创新的企业。阿里巴巴现在的回报是超过一千倍了。我说这个例子给大家听就是要说明其实中国有很多创新的企业是比较有潜力的，但是大家未必能马上能看到它的未来潜力。在这种情况下，新加坡和香港若有这样的国际视野和思维，是否可以投资这些企业——尤其是一些干不下去的企业呢？阿里巴巴和腾讯以前就是干不下去了，但是一旦有人投资，就有所转变了——现在他们都已经发展起来了。新加坡可以成为这样的城市、这样的国家吗？香港可以吗？大家真的可以去考虑这个问题。

我的总结就是，中国现在发展得非常迅速，而且中国的中产阶层和高收入的阶层正迅速地崛起。有报告显示，去年中国的千万富翁已经达到差不多一百六十万，比十年前的十八万人增长了接近九倍，相当于每天有四百人——中国每天有四百人可以成为千万富翁。而且，中国现在有两三亿的中产阶级，有报告说，数据可能会增长到四五亿。反正是有几亿的中产阶级，而且这个数据未来是会进一步扩大的。在这种情况下，新加坡、香港是否需要去关注这几亿的中产阶级？

因此，虽然在中国国内或国外，都有人认为中国的制造业开始往下走了，或认为中国的人口红利已经快开始结束了，但是，事实上中国在金融业，服务业和消费领域的人口红利才刚刚开始。而且，除了中国，世界上再也没有数量如此庞大及明确的市场了。所以，这种商机对于新加坡和香港来说，是非常庞大的，而且大家对于相互之间的文化都是比较了解的。所以，未来新加坡和香港的机遇，可能更多的是在中国。新加坡和香港需要好好地抱握住中国新出现的这种人口的红利。

Democracy in Hong Kong[1]

LAW, Sai Kit Alex

Professor LAW, Sai Kit Alex was born in Hong Kong. He obtained his BSc degree in Physics from Caltech in 1972, and Ph.D. degree in Biology from Harvard University in 1978. After three years at the Washington University Medical School at St. Louis, he joined Professor Rodney Porter's MRC (Medical Research Council) Immunochemistry Unit in the University of Oxford, UK in 1981. He became a full member of the MRC Immunochemistry Unit in 1986. In 2002 he joined Nanyang Technological University in Singapore as a Professor in the School of Biological Sciences (SBS). At NTU, he served as Associate Chair of Research in SBS (2002–2010), Acting Chair of SBS (2008–2011), and the Director of the Double Degree Programme in Biomedical Sciences and Chinese Medicine (2012–2016). His major research work was on proteins of the immune system. He retired at the end of 2016 and now lives in Hong Kong.

According to the Sino-British Joint Declaration of 1984, Hong Kong was to be returned to China on 1 July 1997 to become the Hong Kong Special Administrative Region (HKSAR) of the People's Republic of China (PRC). For the 50 years that followed, HKSAR, as an "inalienable" part of the PRC, was to be administered under the "One Country, Two Systems" principle. The HKSAR government would be able to exercise a high degree of autonomy and enjoy the executive, legislative and independent judicial power. In addition, Hong Kong would be allowed to steer towards democracy in a gradual and orderly manner, with no pre-determined time-line and scope on the move towards democracy. It is therefore appropriate to take stock and assess the progress towards democracy after 20 years into the 50 years span.

Democracy

First, let me make two general points about democracy:

(1) Democracy is not the only acceptable and workable form of government. Indeed, many countries that practice democracy are not doing so well.
(2) Democracy has many versions and different countries would practice their own versions.

I shall also make one point about democracy, specifically on Hong Kong:

(3) Hong Kong is not a country. It is a Special Administrative Region under the People's Republic of China. Democracy in HKSAR can only be operated within this confinement.

Democracy in Hong Kong before 1997

Hong Kong did not have democracy when under the British rule. At a broad stroke, everyone and anyone of significance in government were appointed by the British, officially by the Monarch, and it had been Her Majesty Queen Elizabeth II since her coronation in 1953. This was clearly the situation up till the early 1990s.

Hong Kong became a British colony in three phases. Hong Kong Island (香港岛) was ceded to the British in the Treaty of Nanking after the First Opium War in 1842, followed by the Kowloon Peninsula (九龙半岛) and Stonecutters Island (昂船洲) by the Convention of Peking after the Second Opium War in 1860. The British also acquired the New Territories (新界) through a "lease" under the Convention for the Extension of Hong Kong Territory for 99 years in 1898. The bulk of the New Territories include the land mass adjoining the mainland, and about 400 islands of various sizes, the largest of which is the Lantau Island (大屿山) where the current Chek Lap Kok Airport (赤腊角机场) is located. When we refer to Hong Kong now, it is these combined territories.

In the late 1970s, Deng Xiaoping (邓小平) came to power, and began to steer China away from the accumulated chaos of the Great Leap Forward (大跃进), the Cultural Revolution (文化大革命), and the Gang of Four (四人帮), and onto the path of "recovery". In the historic meeting in 1984 in Beijing, he was able to negotiate with Margaret Thatcher (撒切尔夫人), the Prime Minister of the United Kingdom then, on the return of Hong Kong to China. The formal document was the Sino-British Joint Declaration (中英联合声明), with the main point being the handover of Hong Kong back to China on 1 July 1997. In Deng Xiaoping's view, as well as many Chinese, it was a move to "right the wrongs" of the unequal treaties resulted in the British rule in Hong Kong.

Hong Kong would become a Special Administrative Region of the PRC (中华人民共和国香港特别行政区). The big hurdle was to decide on how HKSAR was to be governed after the handover. It was clear that to parachute the socialist system of China to Hong Kong would be disastrous. Thus the concept of "One Country, Two Systems" (一国两制) was born. Hong Kong was to keep its capitalistic economy and continue with its "modern" lifestyle, which was encapsulated in Deng Xiaoping's own words in Chinese "马照跑, 舞照跳!", with the English translation: "Keep on racing, keep on dancing!"

1. *Hong Kong government structure*

In order to make this article easier to follow, I shall briefly describe the government structure and the political parties of HKSAR. The Head of the HKSAR government is the Chief Executive (行政长官, also colloquially referred to as 特首). He or she is to be elected locally and then appointed by the Central People's Government (中央人民政府).

The Executive Council (行政会议), namely the Government of HKSAR, include the three Departments of Administration, Finance, and Justice, as well as various bureaux, divisions, and commissions. Heads are appointed by the Chief Executive.

The Legislative Council (立法会) is to enact laws and oversee government policies. Members are elected locally. Currently there are 70 members in the Legislative Council.

At present, there are no less than 35 political parties in Hong Kong. These political parties may be divided into three basic camps. In the beginning there were two: the pro-democracy camp, later known collectively as the "pan-democrats", or simply "pan-dems" (泛民), and the pro-establishment camp (建制派). The "pan-dems" pushed for rapid democratization, whereas the pro-establishment camp took a more gradual route and were willing to work with Central Peoples' Government in Beijing. Then in 2015, a splinter camp emerged from the "pan-dems" who wanted to go all-the-way to independence. They are the localists or separatists (本土派). Collectively, together with the "pan-dems", they are now known as the anti-establishment camp (非建制派).

In this article, I will focus on the elections of the Chief Executive and members of the Legislative Council and the stance of the three political camps on these elections as a measure of the progress of democracy in Hong Kong.

2. Basic Law² (基本法) relating to democracy

The Basic Law of HKSAR was devised to provide some guidelines on how Hong Kong was to be run. It was enacted by the National People's Congress (全国人民代表大会) in 1990, and was to be put into effect after its handover on 1 July 1997.

The crux of the Basic Law was to assure, without unequivocal terms, that HKSAR is an inalienable part of the PRC (Article 1), and that HKSAR is to exercise a high degree of autonomy and enjoy the executive, legislative and independent judicial power (Article 2).

3. Selection and election of the Chief Executive and members of the Legislative Council

In addition, Hong Kong was permitted to steer towards democracy. The selection processes of the Chief Executive and members of the Legislative Council may be decided eventually by universal suffrage (Articles 45 and

68). However, if and when the progress of democracy reaches this stage, how the candidates are to be nominated are not spelled out. In addition, no specific target date was set for the implementation of universal suffrage, but with a clause that the progress towards these aims is to be "gradual and orderly" (循序漸進).

It is reasonable not to spell out everything in detail in the Basic Law. The "One Country, Two Systems" is a novel concept of government never tried out anywhere before. Therefore, built-in flexibility features are necessary to give it room to adjust when needed.

4. *The Legislative Council election in 1991*

With the Basic Law in place, Hong Kong, while still a British colony, was able to conduct election for members of the Legislative Council for the first time in 1991. Of the 59 members, 39 were elected (of which 18 were elected from Geographical Constituencies and 21 from Functional Constituencies),[3] 17 appointed by the Governor, and 3 ex-officio (the Chief Secretary, the Attorney General, and the Financial Secretary), with the Governor as President of the Council.

The significance of this election can be seen in three ways: (i) it was the first time that the people of Hong Kong had a vote; (ii) Hong Kong was still under British rule; and (iii) China saw no objection in allowing the election to take place, i.e. the Central People's Government did not object to the move towards democracy.

5. *The accident in the British general election in 1992*

Then there was the "accident" in 1992. There was a general election in the United Kingdom and the Conservative Party won, and John Major (馬卓安) was returned as Prime Minister. Chris Patten (彭定康), who was the Chairman of the Conservative Party, was credited for masterminding the general election win. The accident was that he lost, rather unexpectedly, in his own constituency, Bath. He was therefore not able to retain his seat in parliament.

At the time, David Wilson (衛奕信), as the Governor of Hong Kong, and Percy Cradock (柯利達), as Foreign Affairs Advisor to the Prime

Minister, were heavily involved with the Chinese to iron out the details of the handover. They were judged to have made too many concessions to Beijing. John Major decided to replace David Wilson with Chris Patten, who was to become the Last Governor of Hong Kong. Percy Cradock was later relieved from his positions in the Foreign Office, both as the Foreign Affairs Advisor to the Prime Minister, and as the Chairman of the Joint Intelligence Committee.

6. *Chris Patten's Legislative Council electoral reform in 1994 and its consequences*

Chris Patten pushed for more and immediate democracy, and introduced a series of electoral reforms of the Legislative Council that would include (i) the elimination of the appointments by the Governor, (ii) the expansion of the electoral base; and (iii) the lowering of the voting age from 21 to 18. He succeeded in pushing these changes through government by the narrowest of margins, and these changes were adopted in the Legislative Council Election in 1995.

These changes did not please the Central People's Government in Beijing since Chris Patten apparently did not consult with them. In addition, whereas the election of members of Legislative Council in 1991 was an acceptable "gradual move" towards democracy within the confines of the Basic Law, the reforms put forth by Chris Patten were too abrupt.

Over and over again, it is these undefined terms in the Basic Law that become the contentious points over which the political debates and arguments focus on in later years.

Election of the Chief Executive

The procedure for selecting the first Chief Executive must take place before the handover on 1 July 1997 so that he/she can assume duty immediately. The procedure was spelled out in detail in Annex I of the Basic Law. Briefly, the Election Committee was composed of 800 members representing various sectors in Hong Kong. The Chief Executive was to be elected with a one-person-one-vote by members of this committee. In anticipation of possible changes in the future, as the eventual aim was to have universal suffrage as stated in Article 45, provisions were in place for this method to be amended. However, there would be no change before 2007. After that, amendments could be made, but would require the endorsement of a two-third majority in the Legislative Council, followed by the approval of the Chief Executive, then the approval of the Standing Committee of the National People's Congress (NPCSC，全国人民代表大会常务委员会).

In 2007, the NPCSC ruled out universal suffrage for the election of the Chief Executive of the HKSAR in 2012, but it may be implemented in 2017. In 2010, an amendment was proposed and accepted to have the membership of the Election Committee to expand from 800 to 1200 for the 2012 Chief Executive Election.

1. *Events leading up to the election of the Chief Executive in 2017*

Hong Kong tried to bring universal suffrage for the election of the Chief Executive in 2017, but who would be the candidates? With so many political parties each looking after its own interests, they found no common grounds for a nomination process. A report was made by the Chief Executive to the NPCSC, which handed down its decision on "issues relating to the selection of the Chief Executive of Hong Kong Special Administrative Region by universal suffrage and the method in forming the Legislative Council of the Hong Kong Special Administrative Region in the year 2016". As the decision was dated on 31 August 2014, it is generally referred to as the 831 Decision.

In essence, there will be a 1200 member nomination committee similar to the Election Committee in 2012 to nominate two to three candidates. All eligible voters will have the right to vote for one of the candidates. The successful candidate will have to be appointed by the Central People's Government. It also re-emphasized, as stated in Article 43 of the Basic Law, that the Chief Executive is to be accountable to the Central People's Government and the HKSAR, and extended to spell out the quality of the Chief Executive who "has to be a person who loves the country and loves Hong Kong", and his/her role is "to maintain long-term prosperity and stability of Hong Kong and uphold the sovereignty, security and development interests of the country".

If one examines the 831 Decision document, one would find the following three phrases in the final paragraph. In Chinese, they are "一国两制" (One Country. Two Systems), "港人治港" (Hong Kong people administering Hong Kong) and "高度自治" (high degree of autonomy). And these three phrases have become contentious points of argument for the two sides.

2. *One Country, Two Systems (一国两制)*

Whereas it was understood that the "system" to be operated in HKSAR would not be the same as that in the rest of the PRC, the pro-democracy camp had consistently argued that "two systems" should mean two completely different systems. Anyone can see that "two non-identical systems operating in one country" is not the same as "two completely different systems operating in one country". Whereas the former is comprehensible, the latter makes no sense. If there are "two completely different systems", one might as well have two countries, which points the way to independence — more on that later. Any directive, such as the 831 Decision, would be regarded by the pro-democracy camp as the Central People's Government's interference in HKSAR affairs in violation of the "One Country, Two Systems" principle.

3. *Hong Kong people administering Hong Kong (港人治港)*

This phrase made its appearance in the 831 Decision, but it is not in the Basic Law. What does the word "zhi" (治) mean? It could mean "tongzhi" (统治), "guanzhi" (管制) or "zhili" (治理) which are very different. In English, it could be translated to mean "govern", "rule", and "administer" or "manage" respectively. In the official English translation, it is "... Hong Kong people administering Hong Kong ...". When back-translated into Chinese, it would be "Xianggang ren zhili Xianggang" (香港人治理香港). As a slogan, it is a mouthful. When thrown to the crowd, the short form "gang ren zhi gang" (港人治港) has become a powerful slogan to stir up whatever emotion there is to be stirred up.

4. *High degree of autonomy (高度自治)*

"How high is high?" The Central Government clearly thought that election process outlined in the 831 Decision was "high enough", at least for the Chief Executive Election in 2017. It was a move towards democracy and in line with the pace described as a "gradual and orderly manner". The pro-democracy camp thought otherwise.

However, "high degree of autonomy" immediately suggests that it is not "full autonomy". As previously mentioned, it can only be realised in the context of Hong Kong being an SAR under the People's Republic of China.

5. *Occupy Central (占领中环, or 占中)*

In protest, the pro-democracy camp planned a huge sit-in in the Central District of Hong Kong to demand real universal suffrage. They refused to accept the 831 Decision as a temporary measure in the move towards democracy. They blocked off all traffic in the Central District. At times, the crowd was estimated to be in the order of 100,000. The city was paralysed for 79 days (28 September to 15 December 2014). Road blocks were also set up in Mong Kok, and Causeway Bay.

Their primary slogan was "We want genuine universal suffrage" ("我要真普选"), highlighting the fact that the election method outlined in the 831 Decision did not conform to international standards. I am not quite sure what international standard means as we can find many election formats in different countries. The pro-democracy camp also claimed that once the proposal was accepted, it would remain and stay forever (袋住先，袋一世), i.e. Hong Kong will have no chance to further develop an election of "international standard".

At the height of Occupy Central, there was an open petition organised by the Alliance for Peace and Democracy (保普选保和平大联盟) to call off Occupy Central and it received over 1.8 million signatures. (I was in Hong Kong during the period from 25 October to 2 November, and I registered my support.) The petition was questioned over its credibility (by the pro-democracy camp, of course), and Occupy Central continued until 15 December 2014.

6. *Voting down the electoral reform*

There were more discussions, proposals and counter-proposals in early 2015 to try to work out a consensus plan to bring about universal suffrage for the Chief Executive election. None was forthcoming. The HKSAR government was only able to put up a formal proposal of electoral reform, essentially based on the 831 Decision, to the Legislative Council. A two-third majority was required to approve the proposal. At the end, it was voted down on 18 June 2015, and the election of the Chief Executive in 2017 would be conducted as before, i.e. no universal suffrage.

(On the day, there was chaos in the Legislative Council chamber. Many pro-establishment legislators had left the chamber when it was time to vote. The anticipated result was that the proposal would have a major-ity support but short of the required two-third. Instead, the proposal was officially defeated with 8 votes in favour and 28 votes against.)[4]

7. *The emergence of the localists/separatists and the Mong Kok Riot* (旺角暴乱)

Before Occupy Central, there had been sentiments for the independence of Hong Kong, but they were background noises. After Occupy Central, they emerged from the woodwork. New political parties sprang up and openly advocated for Hong Kong independence.

If Occupy Central was initiated and backed by the "pan-dem" politi-cians, the Mong Kok riot was the work of the localists. With the excuse to fight for the rights of the unlicensed street hawkers who sold fishballs in the traditional Chinese New Year period, the protesters were out in force on Chinese New Year Day 2016. The police, who were there to attempt to maintain some kind of order, soon became the target of the protesters. It was obvious that the protestors had always sought this confrontation. They were very organised and prepared. They wore masks to hide their identities, and they came with home-made shields, which were clearly made in advance. They also came with crowbars to dig out the bricks in the pavement which they used to throw at the police at close range. Several policemen were severely injured.

Although the number engaged in the riot, estimated to be less than 1,000, was substantially less than that of Occupy Central, the severity of the confrontation was much more intense. In less than 24 hours, the num-ber of casualties reached to over 200, accounting for both the police and the protesters.

The Legislative Council Election in 2016 and the Oath-Taking Saga

In the 831 Decision, there was also a ruling on the election of Legislative Council members. The method for forming the fifth term Legislative Council in 2012 was deemed to represent major strides towards democracy, and there was therefore no need to change it for the 2016 election. In addition, the election of all the members of the Legislative Council of HKSAR may be implemented by the method of universal suffrage after the election of the Chief Executive by universal suffrage.

The Legislative Council election was held on 4 September 2016. Several potential candidates were disqualified before the election due to their open stance on supporting Hong Kong independence. However, several had leaked through. Among them were two from the Youngspiration Party (青年新政)[5]: Sixtus Baggio Leung Chung-hang (梁頌恒), and Yau Wai-ching (游蕙禎).

Before they can take their seats in the Legislative Council, the legislator-elects had to take an oath in a swearing-in ceremony, which took place on 12 October 2016. Mr Leung and Ms Yau openly displayed their support for Hong Kong independence, and among other defiant gestures, they deliberately mispronounced "the People's Republic of China" with the clear intent to show disrespect and insult. They were subsequently disqualified and lost their seats in the Legislative Council. After many rounds, their appeal ended with the decision of the Court of Final Appeal on 25 August 2017.[6]

In a sense, it is difficult to lay the blame completely on these young politicians. The Democratic Party, which may be regarded as a representative party of the pro-democracy (and later the anti-establishment) camp, issued a report[7] to mark the 20th anniversary of Hong Kong. Part of it reads: "民主黨既不容許香港走向'一國一制'，亦不支持香港獨立，我們認為應在現時主權框架下，實踐最大程度的自決。" Translated into English: "The Democratic Party will not allow Hong Kong to move towards 'one country, one system'. Nor will we support Hong Kong independence. We believe that we should strive for self-determination to the greatest extent under the current framework of [recognising China's] sovereignty."

This makes an interesting reading. Hong Kong was never under a "one country, one system". The current system is far from a "one system" but it is clearly not two completely different systems. Although it explicitly states that the party does not support Hong Kong independence, the next line says "... we should strive for self-determination to the greatest extent ...". They do want full autonomy (i.e. independence) except in name — so as not to openly challenge Article 1 of the Basic Law. They are not stepping over the bottom line, they are just touching it. These young politicians had simply taken the message of the pro-democracy camp and driven it to the logical conclusion of Hong Kong independence.

However, this is not the whole story. On the day, there were other legislator-elects who did not take their oaths properly, and four more were later disqualified. They have until 11 September 2017 to file an appeal.[8] Hong Kong is now busy organising re-election for the vacated seats.[9]

Progress of Democracy in Hong Kong (1997–2017)

1 July 2017 marked the 20th anniversary of the handover of Hong Kong to China, and the inauguration of the fourth Chief Executive of HKSAR. President Xi Jinping of the People's Republic of China was in Hong Kong to honour the occasion. In the ceremony, speeches were delivered by President Xi and Mrs Carrie Lam, the new Chief Executive of HKSAR. Both speakers used the same two words, in Chinese, "內耗", which gave a precise description of the situation in Hong Kong in the last few years. Roughly translated, they mean internal exhaustion with no purpose. My view is that the move towards democracy has taken a wrong turn. Instead of progress, we are going backwards.

1. *Rushing towards your goal may prevent you from reaching it* (欲速則不达)

Hong Kong did not have democracy under British rule. The British, who left behind a credible civil service, did not prepare the Hong Kong people for democracy. Democracy is not just about giving the people the right to vote. The people have to be prepared to understand that the right to vote comes with responsibilities and consequences.

In 1991, Hong Kong made a first step towards democracy in the Legislative Council election. However, this effort was undone by Chris Patten. Given that the target is to promote democracy in Hong Kong, it is a necessary first step to decide on what type of democratic system would work in Hong Kong. There is no shortage of examples from the many democratic systems practised in different countries of the world. A comparative analysis would show that some will suit Hong Kong better than others. It is also important to recognise that Hong Kong is not an independent country, and the system can only work, at least till the year 2047, under the "One Country, Two Systems" principle. Chris Patten did none of the above. Instead, he simply pushed through large-scale electoral reforms. He had committed the fundamental mistake very well described by the Chinese proverb: "欲速则不达", which can be roughly translated to "rushing towards you goal may prevent you from reaching it". Hong Kong was jumping into democracy without a clear direction.

Encouraged by the Governor, political parties sprang up like "bamboo shoots after the rain in spring" and in Chinese, "雨后春笋". In the 1995 Legislative Council election, the successful candidates came from no less than 15 political parties, each with its own version of how Hong Kong should be run. The general public in Hong Kong may be forgiven for not being able to tell one party from another, let alone their policies and political stance. As an example, there were two political parties called "Hong Kong Confederation of Trade Unions" (香港职工会联盟) and "Hong Kong Federation of Trade Unions" (香港工会联合会) respectively. Incidentally, the former belonged to the pro-democracy camp, whereas the latter the pro-establishment camp. With such confusion, Hong Kong was not ready for democracy in 1997.

The politicians should have sorted this out and consolidated the parties into a manageable number, each with a clear mandate. HKSAR can then move "gradually and orderly" towards greater democracy. But it did not happen. In due course, parties formed and dissolved, split and merged, and their number grew to more than 35 in the 2016 Legislative Council election.

2. *The pro-democracy movement in Hong Kong*

Hong Kong is a Special Administrative Region in the People's Republic of China. The HKSAR government is answerable to the Central People's Government according to the Basic Law. Thus, the Chief Executive and the HKSAR government became easy targets for the pro-democracy camp to accuse of working for the regime of Beijing and selling out the "democratic rights" of the people of Hong Kong.

They take on the role of the opposition. Their complaints are mostly about the "oppression of democracy" and infringement on the promise of the "high degree of autonomy" under the Basic Law. Their actions are mostly organised parades and demonstrations with high visibility. Other than the campaign for the many types of "rights" such as freedom of speech and expression, there is not much substance behind it.

Their complaints about the Central Government's interference on Hong Kong affairs are not justified. If the HKSAR government is accountable to the Central Government, it can only mean that the Central Government has jurisdiction over the HKSAR government. At times, it is necessary for the Central Government to step in to clarify uncertain points over contrasting views of the HKSAR government and its opposition. The 831 Decision on the method of Chief Executive Election is one, and the directive in proper oath-taking[10] is another. There is indeed a "no interference" clause in Article 22 of the Basic Law, but it only applies to departments, provinces, autonomous regions, and municipality under the Central Government, but not the Central People's Government itself.

This interpretation can find support in Article 17 of the Basic Law. In brief, laws enacted by the legislature of HKSAR are not final. They have to be reported to the Standing Committee of the National People's Congress. Any law found not in conformity with the Basic Law may be returned and deemed invalid. The Central Government does have authority over the HKSAR government, it is not interference.

Over the last 20 years, instead of focusing their efforts on working with the government to improve the welfare and livelihood of the Hong Kong people, the pro-democracy politicians and their followers, in the name of promoting democracy, did so by stirring up anti-government and anti-communist (also anti-China) sentiments. In the public arena, they held parades and demonstrations which progressively became more extreme, leading to Occupy Central and the Mong Kok Riot. I really cannot see how these two events can be considered peaceful and non-violent, as claimed by the pro-democracy camp.

With current advanced technology, one can watch the Legislative Council sessions live or their recordings.[11] I watched several of these sessions. Disruptions were commonplace. Verbal disruptions ranged from speaking out of order, to raising queries over the smallest points to lengthy details, to asking pointless and irrelevant questions, to chanting slogans and shouting abuse. There were also physical disruptions. They include the carrying of inappropriate props into chamber, to throwing objects including a glass of water, banana, and ghost money. I fail to see how rational and meaningful discussions can be conducted under these circumstances. Furthermore, these disruptions have the cumulative effect of massive time-wasting. This year, many government programmes did not make their way to the sessions to be properly dealt with.

These politicians have always justified their actions as their right to the freedom of speech and expression. They fail to see that the rights and freedom are not without limits. These rights should not include the right to infringe on the right of others, and the right to incite illegal activities such as massive social unrest and violence. They had clearly stepped over these limits in Occupy Central and the Mong Kok riot. There are also the unwritten boundaries that they should observe, such as they have to act with dignity, integrity, decency, and courtesy. I certainly do not see these qualities in some of them.

Hong Kong was not ready for democracy in 1997. Those who tried to promote democracy had only succeeded in polarising the public opinions and sentiments. Reconciliation between those at the extreme ends becomes difficult if not impossible. What they have achieved is destabilising the foundation of a civilised society. Also under threat are the foundations of government, and the foundations of rule of law. Their primary role in public office to serve people of Hong Kong is taking a backseat at best. Indeed, the Democratic Party has a rule that its members are not allowed to join the government, i.e. to be a member of the Executive branch under the Chief Executive. Those who wish to do so will have to resign their membership. The Democratic Party has actively dissociated themselves from the HKSAR government and moved away from the chance to serve the public directly. In 2017, 20 years after its return to China, Hong Kong is even less ready for democracy.

Given the current system, it is up to the voters of Hong Kong to elect sensible, responsible, and able people to public offices, who will take their job seriously. The next chance will come in the Legislative Council election in 2020. In the meantime, we can only hope that the political situation in Hong Kong does not deteriorate further.

Notes

1. This article is based on the talk delivered in the workshop "Singapore and Hong Kong: Comparative Perspective on the Occasion of the 20th Anniversary of the Handover" (香港回归二十周年: 两座城市的情怀研讨会) in Singapore on 4 September 2017. The Workshop was organised by the Institute of Advanced Studies of the Nanyang Technological University of Singapore. The written article therefore only covers events up to that day. Any related developments on the issues discussed will be included in the endnotes.

2. Any references to the Basic Law of Hong Kong can be found in the following websites: for English, http://www.basiclaw.gov.hk/en/basiclawtext/; for traditional Chinese, http://www.basiclaw.gov.hk/tc/basiclawtext/; and for the simplified Chinese, http://www.basiclaw.gov.hk/gb/basiclawtext/

3. Geographical and Functional Constituencies: There are five geographical constituencies in Hong Kong, each with a number of seats to be voted for by the residents in these demarcated regions: Hong Kong Island (6), Kowloon East (5), Kowloon East (5), New Territories East (9), and New Territories West (9).

   Functional constituencies are professional or special interest groups involved in the electoral process. Generally, eligible voters in a functional constituency are persons engaged in the particular profession or those belonging to a special interest group. At present, there are 30 seats elected in the Legislative Council, from 28 functional groups.

4. Details of the confusion in this voting session can be found in "2014–15 Hong Kong Electoral Reform", available online at https://en.wikipedia.org/wiki/2014%E2%80%9315_Hong_Kong_electoral_reform

5. The Youngspiration party was only formed on 21 January 2015 with about 400 members. It is therefore quite remarkable that they were able to secure two seats in the Legislative Council in the 2016 election.

6. Other than being illegal and in violation of Article 1 of the Basic Law, independence is impossible by many other factors. With reference to the

oath-taking "performance" of the two Youngspiration politicians, it was incomprehension. If they were serious about it, they should realize that being an independent country is not just about declaring independence. International recognition is needed, which means diplomacy. Insulting the next door neighbour was clearly not an act of diplomacy. Incidentally, the neighbour is an international superpower, which also provides the very basic daily necessities, including water and food, to Hong Kong. Furthermore, the way Ms Yau mispronounced the word "republic" may be interpreted as an insult not only to the People's Republic of China, but to all countries with the word "republic" in their names (and there are over 150 countries out of some 200 that have the word "republic" in their official names).

7. Abstracted from "站在历史巨人肩上——民主党对香港与中国关系的回顾及展望", available online at https://drive.google.com/file/d/0B1m5zi ISS9RzN3JUOEZsQ09ObzQ/view;

   The English translation was based on the article published in the South China Morning Post on 11 June 2017, available online at http://www.scmp.com/news/hong-kong/politics/article/2097861/democrats-vow-fight-greatest-self-determination-hong-kong.

8. Two of the four disqualified legislators decided to appeal on 11 September 2017. The other two decided not to, so that they may enter the race for the vacated seats. Under the complicated set of rules, the two on appeal may also participate in the race, pending on the time-line of many relevant events, such as the court hearing of the appeal cases.

9. The date for the re-election for the four vacated seats of the two Youngspiration members and the two disqualified legislators not on appeal is set for 11 March 2018.

10. Oath-taking interpretation: The oath-taking ceremony was a fiasco. Some of the legislators definitely use the occasion to show defiance to the HKSAR government and the Central People's Government. Their oath-taking had many variations, but all had the common theme of lacking sincerity in this solemn ceremony. The "interpretation" of the Basic Law, in my opinion, was forced on the NPCSC to set a proper guideline. The Basic Law just cannot anticipate all the (very imaginative) variations that the legislators can dream up. Perhaps the most extreme case was that of Lau Siu Lai. She read the oath in full, but only at a pace of one syllable every six seconds or so. I urge the reader to view the oath-taking session in full in the web link in footnote 11, and you can decide for yourself if the oaths should be accepted, and whether a directive from the NPCSC was justified.

11. The recordings the Legislative Council sessions for the year 2016–2017 can be accessed at http://www.legco.gov.hk/general/english/counmtg/yr16-20/mtg_1617.htm#toptbl. Recordings of previous years are also linked. Note that the whole oath-taking ceremony can be found in the session on 12 October 2016.

Public and Private Partnerships:

Strategies for the "Belt and Road Initiative"

YAN Houmin

Professor YAN Houmin is Dean of the College of Business and Chair Professor of Management Sciences at City University of Hong Kong. Prior to joining City University, he was a Professor at the Chinese University of Hong Kong. He was the Associate Director and Science Advisor for the Hong Kong Government R&D Center for Logistics and Supply Chain Management Enabling Technologies. He was also a tenured Associate Professor at the School of Management, University of Texas at Dallas. Professor Yan's main research areas are stochastic models, simulations, and supply chain management. He has published extensively in top-tier international journals and has been awarded the Best Paper Prizes by professional societies such as the Production and Operations Management Society (POMS) in 2004 and Institute of Industrial Engineers (IIE) in 2005 and 2012. He consults a number of international and local enterprises. Professor Yan received his B.S. and M.S. from Tsinghua University and his Ph.D. from the University of Toronto.

First of all, let me thank IAS-NTU and particularly Professor Phua, who invited me to participate in this event. I had a conversation with Professor Phua and he wanted me to talk about BRI-related matters. At this point in time, the "Belt and Road Initiative" (BRI), to a certain extent, is a highly attractive topic in Hong Kong; and at the City University of Hong Kong, we have also engaged in BRI-related research and education programmes for some time. So, I would like to share with the audience today our observations on the BRI, its relations with Hong Kong and the roles Hong Kong can play.

At the lunch table, I listened to a conversation about the role Singapore can play in this Chinese central government initiative. I believe over the last few talks we have seen to a certain extent how Hong Kong and Singapore are different, but we also bear some similarities in terms of our economy. Let me go through my slides and I will try to keep to the time given to me.

The first question I would like to ask is, what is BRI? While the central government has well articulated its objectives, in simple words, I would say that this mega initiative is set to promote the following five links. They are policy communication (政策沟通), road connectivity (道路联通), monetary circulation（货币流通）, unimpeded trade (贸易畅通) and understanding between the peoples (民心相通).

Little Ancient Silk Road Facts

After going through this morning's excellent talks by Principal Wang and Alex Law, let me also have a little reflection about the history — the Silk Road history, and I believe many of us have been talking about the different aspects of the Silk Road in history. However, I felt there were a few little details that were not mentioned sufficiently. Let me name you a few. Firstly, the trade. On the ancient Silk Road, not all goods were shipped from China to Europe or to the Middle East or vice versa. Instead, trades were largely local. For instance, out of 100% of the Chinese goods that travelled to Mongolia, 50% was sold along the route, and so 50% was replaced with Mongolian products and this went on continually all the way to Russia and they sold another 50%. So, in reality, commodities on their camels and horses that reached Europe, Chinese products actually made up a smaller percentage than we might think. Therefore, in the success of hundreds of years of Silk Road trade, in addition to the long-distance trade, there was a lot of local trade. So for the present BRI, if we do not get the local countries to participate, it will not be successful. Secondly, the name of "Silk Road". We call it the Silk Road and many people believed it is due to the Chinese silk shipped to Europe. Yes, but it is not in the form of finished goods but rather in bolts of silk as a means of payment. Because it is light weighted but high in value, at that point in time, silk was a currency, a means of payment and finance. These little pieces of history shed light on how the Silk Road was running and some key factors contributing to its trade volume.

Public Private Partnerships for Infrastructure Projects

The Silk Road concept was revived with the BRI proposed by President Xi. Given its geopolitical nature, ambitious scope and vast scale, people tend to compare the BRI with the 50-year Marshall Plan and 5-year Yonkers Plan. Of course, those plans were conceptualised in different time periods, aiming to deal with different economic and political situations. As I am from a business school, I will look into their financial aspect. According to different statistics and reports, the money which is needed for the BRI is going to be huge and there are institutions newly formed in China with the participation of many international organisations. They set up the Asian Infrastructure Investment Bank (AIIB) and they also have the Silk Road Fund, China's new development banks, the BRICs funding and many more. But if you really look into the bidding of funding, while the requirement for those projects is huge, the support from a few countries and the financial situation of these institutions are not that promising.

More flexible financing and management models for BRI projects are therefore needed. There is a business model known as Public Private Partnership (PPP) that is basically trying to leverage the private side of the money with the need of the public service. These public private partnership projects cover highways, electricity, water supply and many other dimensions. The idea is that the public and private sectors leverage their own strengths. The public sector has a need to promote infrastructure projects or needs to implement its own projects, and the private sector has money and often the expertise. Through collaboration, the public sector is able to manage risk at home country by means of legislation, and mitigate or shoulder political risk (such as currency inconvertibility and transfer restriction, expropriation, breach of contract, political violence, legal, regulatory and bureaucratic risks, etc.) through diplomatic action or bilateral agreements. And the private sector has much of the required resources, and often have better operational efficiency than governmental/public organizations. So that was the basic idea. However, different countries may have different objectives for adopting PPPs. In developing countries, they may be looking for private funding. In developed countries, they may aim at better efficiency. In under-developed countries, they may look for both funding and expertise/technology. The ultimate goal is to exercise strengths and make things better.

If one were to look into a particular PPP project, usually there is a special purpose company as part of the project agreement, which is a separate entity from the government formed specifically to undertake that specific project. Financial arrangements can be relatively sophisticated. You can have investors as well as people willing to provide money. Therefore, in order to make a particular PPP project successful, you would probably want to look into a particular project cycle, starting with the legislative requirements, continuing with project identification and looking into project procurement from the government's side and continuing with project design and development, and after the completion of the project, it will probably involve the implementation and operation for a defined period as well.

A particular example from Hong Kong is MTR, the Mass Transit Railway. While MTR operates the city's railway, charging a relatively low fares, it does not require Hong Kong government subsidies. How is this achieved? For the underground railway development, Hong Kong government has given MTR Corporation concessions, providing the company with the operation right of the new rail line as well as the land development right of the site. While building the new rail line, MTR partners with private developers to complete new residential and commercial properties atop the MTR station site. By capturing part of the value of the land property around railway lines, MTR generates funds for new projects as well as for operations and maintenance. That is a varied form of the PPP model.

In terms of business sectors, we believe that infrastructure development might be a promising area for BRI projects. Moreover, infrastructure projects will probably be associated with all the five-links which I just mentioned before. Recently, I was invited to conduct a benchmarking exercise for the NDRC (The National Development and Reform Commission of the People's Republic of *China)* on its BRI PPP projects and I had a deeper look into those 50 projects and their sectors, which involves highways, power, garbage management, water supply and other large-scale public facilities.

Benchmarking of PPP Projects

If you look into the countries which those projects are taking place, many of them are Southeast Asian countries. As I mentioned earlier, in order to have those projects successful, a primary factor is the regulatory framework. Investors need to take a closer look into whether the local laws allow people to carry out with those projects and to implement the operations thereafter. Nonetheless, some Southeast Asian countries may not yet have their regulatory framework ready, and the situation is not that ideal if you look at countries, like Cambodia and Myanmar, which are still at their developing stage. Let me jump to the World Bank's Benchmarking PPP Procurement 2017 exercise. It is a three-year long project conducted by the World Bank as the first attempt to collect and present comparable and actionable data on PPP procurement on a large scale. They looked into those projects from different perspectives — legislative, financial, and operational. They looked at 82 economies and they found out that there were indeed specific framework for regulating PPPs. 50% of the countries are wasting its system. On the other hand, there are other countries which are at different stages to support that type of actions. But if you look into small details, different economies perform differently in several dimensions like PPP procurement process, contract management and legislative matters for PPP projects.

ECA is Europe and Central Asia, EAP is East Asia Pacific, OECD (Organisation for Economic Co-operation and Development) are those developing countries, SAR is the South Asia region. It turns out that Southeast Asia is not that bad compared to the rest of the world.

Further looking into Southeast Asia and taking China into consideration, PPP procurement, PPP legislation and contracts management are the areas in which Southeast Asia is doing quite well. So that's why, to a certain extent the speakers this morning had also mentioned that Hong Kong and Singapore, probably in view of their legal environment, or their economic position, can play a certain important role in the BRI. If you look into the World Bank's three-year study, it mentions that even countries like the Philippines have very sophisticated PPP policies, which provide assurance in terms of the legal and regulatory framework because legal environment is definitely an important determinant for investing or participating in a PPP related project or not.

Operational Strength

Next, let me try to introduce Hong Kong as an example. We will see how Hong Kong's business community or companies could play in this important central government initiative. In Hong Kong, we never talk about BRI collaborations or Greater Bay Area development. However, if you talk to the government officials or just an ordinary Hong Kong people, the first two things they will tell you are: First, Hong Kong has a sound financial system; and second, Hong Kong has a good legal system. I believe that those two things are true. But on the other hand, if you were looking into Hong Kong's so-called financial system, Hong Kong has close to 180 foreign banks. However, there is only one from the BRI countries. If you look at Hong Kong's legal system, it is based on common law, but if you look around the BRI countries, they probably do not use common law nor continental law. Surely, Hong Kong has strengths in finance and legal systems. However, those two areas still need further tune-up in order for Hong Kong to play a significant role in the BRI. And I would like to speak loudly on the other advantage that Hong Kong has, and that is its versatile operations. Looking at Hong Kong's history, what Hong Kong companies did best in the past. If you are looking at companies like Li & Fung, back in the old days, when they were doing the trade; basically, they were operators, they were agents. They knew where to source materials, which company produced good garments; which company did good designs and cutting, and they also knew where to find customers. Therefore, Hong

Kong companies, to a certain extent, are good operators. Again, looking into construction and infrastructure sector of Hong Kong, I hope that you will be convinced that Hong Kong people has a great advantage in being operators.

Quoting the MTR example again. There is no doubt that a city needs railways. Because it is faster, it takes up lesser land, it is massive. In addition, it is energy efficient, has low carbon emissions, helps promote economic growth in the region. Everything is good. But if you look at the investment, you need a huge initial capital investment and the on-going maintenance cost. After a few years of operation, the maintenance costs will go up as well. Therefore, if you really want to invest in the railway systems, according to MTR's estimation, the annual return is 1.5%. Nobody wants to invest in that kind of business with such a low return. Because if you do nothing and just put money in the bank and you might get more than 1.5%. But, there is a public need, a need to build railway systems for efficient public transportation. So, what does Hong Kong deal with this? Real estate is a hot topic in Hong Kong today. It turns out that real estate is key to financing this kind of projects. In Hong Kong, location is a primary factor affecting real estate prices, and the price of any apartment above a railway station is significantly higher than in other places. The Hong Kong MTR took this advantage and said that they have a way to do the project. It is "rail plus property" model. And look, this property development is another way to get private funding — more than just one or two, three, five investors but ordinary people, like you and me, all actively participate as private investors in those projects. Therefore, according to Hong Kong MTR, this rail plus property model is a win-win strategy. On the one hand, we have the railway that adds value to the property. On the other hand, the government, society and even the economy all benefit from the rail development.

Here are some basic statistics. President Wang was here this morning, and at that time travelling to The University of Hong Kong was troublesome. The West Island Rail Line brought a big difference to the district. People talked about the Occupy Central, saying that the students took the subway to attend classes in the university during the day and participated in Occupy Central in the evening. That was a joke. The line was put in service after Occupy Central, if I remember correctly. Look at the subway that used to stop at Sheung Wan, now extended to Sai Ying Pun to Hong Kong University and Kennedy Town. Even with only these three stations of extension, there is huge value generated for the region, and the accumulated benefits, both tangible and intangible, for the government. For example, incomes from the rates and stamp duty are all bidding of the dollars. Therefore, when assessing investments into big infrastructure projects, I believe that this is something that we can learn from.

Actually, MTR is expanding its operations and it is very much on purpose in doing this extension. Now, Hong Kong MTR is running rail operations in China. If you cross to Shenzhen, Shenzhen subway number 4 is operated by MTR. If you go to Beijing, subway number 4 in Beijing is also operated by MTR. Farther away, MTR is also running a business in places like New Zealand, Australia and recently in the UK. It is not only MTR expanding its overseas operations. I was told that a semi-government corporation, Hong Kong Airport Authority (HKAA), is building the third runway with a team of 1,200 professionals. Here comes the question: After the third runway is done, are we going to lay off all the 1,200 experienced professionals that have worked on the runway? Or are we expanding and going overseas? What I am trying to say is that, in addition to financial and legal systems, in Hong Kong we do have the expertise to put on the table. That is what I mentioned earlier, our operational strength. I am sure that there are also other professional services that economies like Hong Kong and Singapore can provide when taking part in the BRI.

PPP Research and Training at City University of Hong Kong

I know my time is almost up. Please allow me to do a little bit of propaganda. In Hong Kong, many things are quite political. If you read the *Ming Pao* editorial on 31 July which talks about the Japanese Prime Minister Abe's economic policies. At the end, the editorial asks, why does the Hong Kong government actively develop new policies in response to the initiative crisis instead? That said, for the BRI and the Greater Bay Area projects as well, I doubt if Hong Kong businesses and higher educational institutions contribute enough. So, I am doing a bit of propaganda in the last few slides. We at the City University has formed a research centre on BRI in September 2015 and a Public Private Partnership China Centre with Tsinghua University in January 2016, which came under the agreement between the United Nations and the NDRC. Among other things, we are trying to strengthen our human capital and we have started sending our students to the United Nations, on training programmes on sustainable PPPs and BRI strategies. We hosted the first United Nations Public Private Partnership workshop at the City University, which covered topics such as People-first PPP projects, PPP standards and how we can carry out PPP projects. We also help NDRC do the benchmarking for the BRI projects. There are many things that has been done at the university level and we plan to introduce new programmes at the master's level, which will train professionals for the BRI PPP related projects. The BRI not only opens up unprecedented opportunities for businesses, but also challenging research opportunities for academia, and I look forward to seeing more research outputs from colleagues all over the world, in the BRI and PPP areas.

Potential and Inertia in the Development of Hong Kong and Singapore:

The Next 20 Years*

YANG Jinlin

Mr. YANG Jinlin, founder of Yang Jinlin New Media, was born in Xiamen, Fujian in 1953. Graduated from the History Department of Xiamen University.

Mr. Yang worked as a chief editorial writer and editor-in-chief among a number of newspaper agencies in Hong Kong. In 2002 Mr. Yang joined the Phoenix Satellite Television and hosted several popular television shows. Among these, *You Bao Tian Tian Du* won China's best television program and most creative show in 2003, as well as the Annual Respected Television Program of Southern Weekly; *Zou Du Da Zhong Hua* won the Most complementary program in the year of 2010.

Mr. Yang joined Hong Kong TV International Media Group in 2011. In January 2013, Mr. Yang founded Yang Jinlin New Media, a Hong Kong-based company with a focus on mainland China market. It has built partnerships with major Chinese online media platforms and TV stations. The programs have received a total of approximately 400 million unique visitors and 800 million page views.

---

* This is a translated version of the original speech in Mandarin.

Good afternoon, ladies and gentlemen. This is the second invitation I received to participate in similar events in Singapore. Thanks for the introduction made by Professor Chen Kang, the invitation from Professor K.K. Phua and thanks to all my old friends for your support.

My speech will not be a discussion of feelings and patriotism, as previous speakers have left nothing for me to explore on that topic. What I will talk about is the potential and inertia for Hong Kong and Singapore. And I believe it will be an interesting topic. I want to talk about the next two decades, and at the same time, I also want to give a retrospective look at the history of both cities. We can make a comparison between the films advertising Hong Kong and Singapore. Hong Kong is an oriental pearl, a glamour city, according to its advertisements. In contrast, Singapore is a garden city, a deeply impressive lion city, again according to its advertisements.

My speech will cover four issues: the first is the historical evolution of Hong Kong and Singapore; the second is the comparison of the core competitive advantages of Hong Kong and Singapore; the third is the potential and inertia of the development of Hong Kong in the next 20 years, from here we can learn the comparability of Singapore and Hong Kong; the fourth is the possible interaction between Hong Kong and Singapore in the future. At the end of this speech, I will share some of my thoughts and feelings with all of you.

I believe you are not unfamiliar with the historical evolution of Hong Kong and Singapore. These two cities, although essentially different in terms of governance, share the same experience of colonisation, endured the same course of economic transformation after the Second World War and have been two of the four small dragons of Asia for quite a few years. The difference between them is, Singapore is an independent nation, while Hong Kong has been returned to China. Their political systems are completely different, and hence, we shall not discuss it here. Judging by core-competitiveness, there is no significant gap in GDP growth rate when comparing Hong Kong and Singapore between 1997 and 2016. There was only a slight drop in Hong Kong's GDP in that period.

Both Hong Kong and Singapore rank within the top five global financial centres. Though there were fluctuations in their rankings, Singapore has been moving up the ranks. Today, Mr Antony Leung Kam-Chung mentioned "狮城领跑" or "the lion city is leading" in his speech. For the word "领跑" or "leading", I think his interpretation should be the same as ours. In Singapore, the economic weight of the manufacturing sector is quite heavy, and the opposite is true for Hong Kong. Singapore is not merely a financial and trade centre as famous as Hong Kong, it spends a great amount of time and effort in the development of science, technology and manufacturing as well. In reality, it has spent more time and effort in these sectors than the service industry. With petrochemical engineering, electronics, machinery as well as biological and pharmaceutical sciences as its four main pillar industries, Singapore is not only regarded as the third largest refinery centre and petrochemical centre in the world, it is also the largest manufacturer of oil drilling platforms. Moreover, Singapore is the largest independent city in the world. In terms of strategic planning, Singapore has a long-term vision with greater depth, breadth and scope than Hong Kong.

From this angle, we are aware that there is a fluctuation in trading and Hong Kong's current cargo handling capacity has been overtaken by Yantian and Xiayang ports. Hong Kong's competitive advantage in entrepôt trade has been declining, while Singapore still has its advantage in this field. As an economic entity, Hong Kong, this micro city with a complex society, is governed by a relatively small government. Although its economy has faced ups and downs, Hong Kong has been one of the freest market economies in the world till present. However, from 1984 to 2017, Hong Kong has not resolved one of its most important problems, the hollowing-out of the real economy. For the so-called "shop at the front and factory production at the back" phenomenon, there are two main historical reasons for the development of this economic pattern. Firstly, there was no necessity for the Hong Kong British authority to make long-term plans for Hong Kong's development as Hong Kong would be returned to China in 1997. Secondly, it is the result of the natural flow of market economies. This kind of economic pattern eventually caused a relative deficit in scientific and technical innovation, which is a serious disadvantage for Hong Kong. In 1997, the first government of the Hong Kong Special Administrative Region proposed to develop Hong Kong as a "digital harbour" and "Chinese herb harbour". However, today, the previously proposed "digital harbour" is actually dominated by the real estate industry. Few high-tech industry players have entered Hong Kong. The high-tech talents nurtured by universities in Hong Kong are employed by either Singapore enterprises or Foxconn. Alternatively, these talents choose to work in Taiwan or Korea. We can see Hong Kong is not attractive for talents. Even if such talents remained in Hong Kong, most of them either gather in finance and real estate, or real estate and finance.

Without the real economy, the long-term development of a free economy will come under threat. It is impossible to support sustainable economic development through sole reliance on the finance, services and tourism industries. That is worrisome for Hong Kong. With regard to this point, Singapore's advantage in leading long-term economic development is obvious.

The second issue I will explore is the potential and inertia of the development of Hong Kong in the next 20 years. Firstly, China will keep the "One Country, Two Systems" policy unchanged for 50 years, which was originally proposed by Mr Deng Xiaoping. After listening to all the speeches this morning, I felt deeply moved and shared my thoughts with Mr Wang Gungwu in the afternoon that two names appeared quite often in these speeches — the first name was Deng Xiaoping, the second was Lee Kuan Yew. That means our discussions on the two cities' fate in the present and future is based on the insights and foresight of these two late leaders. From their vantage point, they had great vision! Keeping the "One Country, Two Systems" policy unchanged for 50 years, in reality, there are only 30 years left now — and Mr Deng said there was no need to change this policy after 50 years either. In fact, changes are already there, for example, economic changes.

Hong Kong's economic development has been on an upward trend from 1997 to 2016, and there is no large-scale unemployment. Even though house prices make housing unaffordable for most people, and the channel for upward social mobility is heavily-obstructed, and class consolidation makes it impossible to recreate the social mobility experienced in the early years of the rise of the bourgeoise in the 1970s and 1980s, the employment rate in Hong Kong has not been fundamentally affected. House prices may be too high for ordinary folk to afford, but it is not necessary for us to protest on the streets. I really want to enjoy hot pot in Admiralty, that is one of my dreams in life. Practically speaking, we cannot put aside the rule of law when discussing ways of expressing political consciousness and participation of a young man.

Let us examine the four major industries of Hong Kong from an economic point of view. For the logistics industry and trade, it has been in decline; for tourism, it is not bad, but not as prosperous as we might think. And the situation of professional services, like accounting and legal services, is ambiguous. The so-called six competitive industries of Hong Kong are not performing as well as we wish. Despite there being six great universities and high-tech innovation industry, the lack of sets of competitive flagship products with unique advantages is the main problem that Hong Kong is facing at present. If we examine the proportion of individual industries' growth relative to total GDP, it is easy to see the consolidation of the industrial structure. There is no new industry entering the mix and upgrading. The development of key industries is static rather than advancing by leaps and bounds.

Here, we will not further explore the historical transition of Hong Kong with the promise of keeping the status quo for 50 years. We will reflect upon the fluctuation of opinion polls for Hong Kong's Chief Executives in recent years. It is really a precious freedom that we can criticise the Chief Executive of Hong Kong at present. The opinion polls reflect a lot of ups and downs which indicate that the recovery of political consciousness and participation has diversified since 1997. That diversification has brought about many challenges for the "One Country, Two Systems" policy, like the Occupy Central event in which protesters occupied Central for 79 days, twice or thrice longer than the June 4, 1989 Incident in Beijing. It demonstrates that Hong Kong has, based on a legal framework, the ability to bear political pressure. It has the ability to deal with a potentially explosive populist and unexpected political participation. This is quite an accomplishment.

In the 1980s, when dealing with the transfer of Hong Kong's sovereignty, the Chinese central government set three strategic targets for Hong Kong: 1. to be a model for Taiwan; 2. to act as a channel to the world; 3. to act as a source of funds. Time passed, and 20 years later, we no longer hear the call for Hong Kong as a model for Taiwan. During the early period of Hong Kong's return, mainland China was still closed off from the rest of the world, as reform and opening-up had just started up.

At that time, Hong Kong was an unimpeded channel connecting China and the world. However, this channel is no longer as important as before. As we know, even a mayor of a village in northwest China can bring a large group to have an investigation trip abroad; there is no longer any need for Hong Kong to be the middleman.

Mainland China is the second largest economy, and its foreign exchange reserves rank top in the world. The party chairman, as well as the president of China, are anxious about what to do with such a large amount of money. So, as a source of funds, as Hong Kong is still famous for high-quality financial services, its advantage lies in its role in reallocating high-quality resources. Mainland China no longer needs funds from Hong Kong. The three strategic targets for Hong Kong set by the central government around 1997 have basically disappeared or dwindled. The situation is compounded by misconception on the part of some Chinese leaders in the early 1980s which has positioned Hong Kong as an economic city, for example, the central government allowed horse racing and nightclubs in Hong Kong when those were prohibited on the mainland. Hong Kong just needed to pay close attention to making money and had no need to be concerned about any other things — that was the idea the central government had about Hong Kong. The important task of decolonising Hong Kong was far from being complete. Under the Basic Law, Hong Kong people administer Hong Kong and have a high degree of autonomy. With the public consciousness of political participation at a new high, Hong Kong people seek greater participation in society and more control over their fate.

We can see that the generation which witnessed Hong Kong's return has a strong sense of political participation, with people who support Hong Kong's independence as the extreme representation of that generation. Today, posters with texts supporting Hong Kong's independence can even be found in the campus of The Chinese University of Hong Kong. It has been 20 years since Hong Kong's return in 1997, but why are there still demands for Hong Kong's independence and a sense of alienation among the Hong Kong people? This problem is rooted in feelings. Education, especially education regarding identities, as carried out by the government of the Hong Kong Special Administrative Region, has gone awry and has resulted in negative consequences similar to that of the de-sinicisation education carried out by the Taiwanese government under Lee Teng-hui and Chen Shui-bian's leadership. This has left a vacuum in attempts to get Hong Kong people to identify with China after Hong Kong's return. How can you expect the youth of this generation — who have received western education and who now find increasingly greater amounts of information about the severe and pervasive nature of corruption among government officers in everyday newspapers — to accept this kind of government and identify with the corresponding culture and value system? After 20 years of political transformation, this is the current state of affairs in Hong Kong. Such an explosive growth in the sense of political participation and the manner of expressing political consciousness form part of a violent, mob-like democratisation phase that is foreign to us and thus, we are incapable of making and passing accurate judgement on this phenomenon. Regarding Hong Kong's social problems, although Chinese President Xi Jinping mentioned that seeking broad common ground and setting aside major differences is a very important tenet, not every individual and department leader has embraced this idea.

The role Hong Kong plays in economic development has obviously been weakened by the rise of Shenzhen. The current night view of Shenzhen is not inferior to that of Hong Kong, the so-called oriental pearl. As Shenzhen's total GDP almost catches up with or even overtakes Hong Kong's, and the structure of the high-tech industry, the entrepreneurial environment as well as facilities in Shenzhen are far better than those in Hong Kong, the integration development between Shenzhen and Hong Kong has been put on the agenda.

The GDP growth of other first-tier cities, such as Beijing, Shanghai and Guangzhou, has been fast as well and Hong Kong has not displayed the advantages it should have had in this respect. Now, let us talk about the future, especially in the next 20 years of Hong Kong and we have a lot of expectations here. Just as previous analysis has shown, Hong Kong's status has gradually changed after its return to mainland China. We can see Hong Kong's advantage in economic development, but at the same time, we also find similar rapid development in the neighbouring areas, such as Shenzhen and Guangdong, as well as in other central cities, such as Beijing, Shanghai, Guangzhou. The three strategic targets for Hong Kong set in the early days of its return have changed with time.

Mr Lee Kuan Yew commented in 1996 that Hong Kong needed an independent and decisive chief executive as well as the assistance of efficient civil servants with clean hands to sustain the British system, the legal system, the solemnity of contract law, as well as the principle of fair commerce and an environment encouraging fair competition. We should reflect on Mr Lee's comments today and check whether these advantages are still applicable.

Do we have an independent and decisive chief executive? Have there been changes in the system of efficient civil servants with clean hands? Has the British legacy of the most efficient and incorruptible legal system in Hong Kong become impaired? Has there been any change in the fair principles governing commerce and the environment of fair competition? Song Lin, the former chairman of China Resources, who was also the chairman of the Hong Kong Independent Commission Against Corruption, was himself charged with corruption. What can we learn from the paradox of Song Lin's case? We can see that Hong Kong's legal system maintains its dignity and credibility, so anyone who commits an offence will be punished by the law. For example, ex-chief executive Donald Tsang was sentenced to prison. In this, we can see Hong Kong's legal system has dealt fairly with members of the Legislative Council of the Hong Kong Special Administrative Region who did not obey the law. We can see the unflagging spirit of the rule of law in Hong Kong, but we can also find some changes in it. During the first three years after Hong Kong's return in 1997, under the policy of "One Country, Two Systems", mainland officers from the level of section chief and above were not allowed to enter Hong Kong; but today, any businessman who offends mainland law can be arrested and sent to the mainland, like the Causeway Bay Books incident. Although ordinary Hong Kong people may not understand the reasons behind this event, they may worry if the spirit of the rule of law continues to be respected and protected in Hong Kong.

I think no matter what kind of changes happen in Hong Kong, it is impossible to change the nature of Hong Kong as a Special Administrative Region of the People's Republic of China. The rapid rise of China has greatly changed the relationship between the two systems, as well as the relationship between Hong Kong and South China or the whole mainland. Whether the "One country, Two systems" policy results in success in Hong

Kong depends not only on the Hong Kong people themselves, but also on a successful modernisation of mainland China, the motherland. There is a view that "One Country, Two Systems" is a fusion of an advanced system and a lagging system rather than a marriage between them. From the perspective of a system, Hong Kong should be regarded as a bridge to connect China and the world. We should not simply think of socialism in mainland China as the laggard that hinders Hong Kong's development. The problem with this view is that it separates the discussion from the historical background in which China asserted sovereignty over Hong Kong using the "One Country, Two Systems" policy in the 1980s. At that time, China was a poor and backward country practising a brand of socialism which had no attraction for people in Hong Kong, Taiwan, Macau or any other overseas Chinese populations at all. That is why the central government adopted the "One Country, Two Systems" policy with a down-to-earth attitude when it regained sovereignty over Hong Kong, to solve a historical problem and it is the first commitment made by the Communist Party of China to international society, which was widely accepted by the world community. Although this policy is not perfect due to the limitation of the times, it is still an objective recognition of the differences between two social systems at that time under the inviolable premise of the unification of Hong Kong and mainland China. It shows respect for the significant difference between two social systems — one being laggard socialism and the other, relatively advanced capitalism, especially in relation to politics and culture.

I think, firstly, this is a progressive move that is truly worthy of affirmation and represents an unprecedented commitment to the international community made by CCP since its foundation. Secondly, China has become rich after 40 years of economic reform, and you can find people with iPhones in hand at every corner of the land — even the amounts involved in bribery can reach as high as tens of millions. With great economic growth, you can find Chinese tourists everywhere in the world. In Paris, you can see Chinese tourists holding several LV bags and talking loudly while walking by. This struck a deep chord in me as we Chinese suffered starvation not long ago. Currently, the Chinese people who enjoy such good lives, can hold their heads up and pay using credit cards without concerns, and it is a real blessing. However, you must admit that in terms of law and order, incorrupt governance, values and ideology, there are significant differences between China and the western world that is the source of the long-term contradiction and friction between Hong Kong and the motherland. Fifty years later, so long as Hong Kong still exists as a special administrative region rather than a district under Shenzhen, this contradiction will remain.

The economic interactions between Hong Kong and mainland China will be closer in the next 20 years. The role of Hong Kong will no longer be that of a unique economic leader which it was previously. Instead, its function will be regionalisation. We can tell this from the development of the Greater Bay Area. The central government's work report clearly indicates that the Greater Bay Area is specifically for the development of Hong Kong and Macau. Although there are four municipalities and five autonomous regions directly under the Central Government, Hong Kong and Macau, the two special administrative regions are the key areas. In the development process envisioned in the plan, some unique advantages of certain regions will be weakened, and some will be strengthened, while some will be restricted. For example, is it possible to put Article 27 of the Basic Law into a discussion agenda? And what would be the reaction of extreme segments of Hong Kong society to it? What will be the reaction of these segments of society to issues of political security and national defence? Some will continue to be restricted and will be hindered by human factors. These are the challenges we should pay attention to and must face. In the foreseeable future, it is impossible to change the nature of Hong Kong as a special administrative region of the PRC. This is a limitation that we cannot break through in the next 20 years.

There is a CIA research report on the 32 possible scenarios of Taiwan independence by CIA, which the secretary-general of the National Security Council of Taiwan, Su Qi, once showed me. We are uncertain if they did research on the possibility of Hong Kong's independence as well. According to this thorough research, there is a common premise for all the 32 possible scenarios, that is the independence of Taiwan must receive the approval of mainland China. This is the scope as well as the limit of the relationship between Taiwan and the mainland, and these boundaries cannot be breached. And there is no need to strive for unrealistic expectations or to fantasise about breaching of these limits, unless there is political upheaval in mainland China. Hong Kong is gradually transforming into a global Chinese city, and is in competition with Shenzhen and Guangdong. From entrepôt to super liaison, it is more and more difficult for Hong Kong to do business and even harder if it cannot provide service with good attitudes.

Such potential and inertia, as I stressed above, determine the next 20 or 30 years for Hong Kong as well as the scope and limitations of its relationship with Singapore, in terms of cooperation, communication and interaction.

What role will Hong Kong play in the next 20 years? Firstly, Hong Kong will be the frame of reference for China's efforts in developing and modernising its legal system, clean governance, entrepreneurial spirit and fair competition. Secondly, it will be an exemplar of sloppy patriotism. Currently, the emphasis is on loving the motherland and Hong Kong. Mr Liao Chengzhi once severely criticised the officers from Unified Front Work and called for all overseas Chinese, including Taiwan, Hong Kong and Macao compatriots, to love the motherland. Loving the motherland does not equate to loving any political party and there is no need to be too strict about it. What does "sloppy patriotism" mean? That means, as a Chinese, I hope my motherland is strong and prosperous regardless of which party is in power. If you can meet the criteria of this "sloppy patriotism", you are a great patriot. This is the most extensive unified front; that is fewer enemies and as many friends as possible, which according to Chairman Mao was the right way to conduct politics.

President Xi Jinping stressed that we should seek broad common ground while setting aside major differences, and "One Country, Two Systems" embodies precisely this tenet. However, does everyone have such magnanimity, compassion and foresight? A single President Xi Jinping is quite far from enough.

The last point is about the first trials of political participation and the democratisation process in Hong Kong, regardless of the type of democracy, whether orderly, procedural or substantial. Hong Kong has the qualities to try the process of democratisation first, even if populism, political demands for Hong Kong independence, and street politics appear in this process. I think all of these can be viewed as a frame of reference for China in its modernisation efforts. This may be a good experience or a good lesson. I am not sure if someone else had talked about Hong Kong's role in the future from this perspective. I think such a role for Hong Kong really exists.

Now, we will talk about the imaginations of Hong Kong and Singapore in 20 years. The next 20 years for Hong Kong and Singapore, in terms of imaginative space, is much larger than it was in the previous 20, 40 or 60 years. The relationship between Hong Kong and Singapore will be affected by international competition but should still be maintained as a partnership. Hong Kong will continue to be an imaginary enemy for Singapore. The difference between their political systems means that it is impossible for both to have interaction as active as before. Their relationship will be affected by many uncertain factors, such as international developments, the situation in the Asia-Pacific Region and the influence of mainland China. The essential factor for Hong Kong maintaining its glamour is its ability in keeping its basic character as the Pearl of the Orient; its original social system, its clean governance, wealth and efficient civil service; and keep up with the expectations outlined by Mr Lee Kuan Yew previously. If Hong Kong completes its transformation into another Chinese city ahead of plans, there will be no need to continue the comparison between it and Singapore. Singapore should pick another Chinese city, such as Shanghai, Guangzhou or Shenzhen, to set up a new comparison.

If Hong Kong's unique characteristics were to be extinguished today, as Mr Ambrose King pointed out, it will either be marginalised or lose its competitiveness. That is not what Chinese leaders would like to see, neither would Singapore leaders wish to witness that, I believe.

I would like to use the words of Liu Guoshen, president of the Taiwan Research Institute of Xiamen University to conclude my speech. Regarding the Taiwan issue, Mr Liu said, the ultimate solution of the Taiwan issue depends on the development of mainland China. He pointed out that mainland China must be clear about the fact that the Taiwanese are afraid and distrustful of the socialist system as well as the Chinese Communist Party, which is an objective fact. The ultimate solution of the Taiwan issue depends on the development of mainland China. Please replace "Taiwan" with "Hong Kong" here, and change "jurisprudential independence of Taiwan" to "jurisprudential independence of Hong Kong", and the same logic applies.

双城记的未来二十年——香港与新加坡发展的高度与限度

杨锦麟

这是我第二次受邀到新加坡来参加类似的活动。感谢陈抗教授的引荐，感谢潘国驹教授的邀请，同时也感谢包括刘宏先生在内的老同学、老朋友前来捧场。

我的题目不谈情怀，因为之前有那么多的讲者已经把情怀说透了。我谈未来二十年，新加坡与香港双城发展的高度和限度。

以下几个问题是我要谈的重点：第一，香港和新加坡的历史沿革；第二，香港和新加坡核心竞争力的比较；第三，香港未来二十年发展的高度和限度——如此一来，我们就知道新加坡的可比性在哪里；最后我要谈的是对双城未来互动的想像。此外，我还有一些感想和大家分享。

历史沿革大家都很熟悉了。虽然新加坡和香港的政治治理形态有本质差异，但两者都经历过相同的殖民统治，有着相似的战后发展经验，也有着类似的经济转型经验，而且它们多年来共享着亚洲四小龙光彩。当然二者也有不同之处，一个是回归，一个是独立。回归与独立之后两者的政治形态和治理方式完全不同。就核心竞争力来看，也就是 GDP 的增长来看，两者在1997到2016年期间的情况其实不相上下，只是香港的跌幅会比新加坡稍微多一点。

香港和新加坡都位居全球金融中心前五名。虽然两者的排名次序都有些变化起伏，但新加坡的排名正在往前走。今天梁锦松先生谈到"狮城领跑"，我想对于"领跑"这两个字，梁先生可能与我们有着相似的解读。工业在新加坡的经济中占有很大的比重，而香港却恰恰相反。新加坡不仅拥有可以媲美香港的金融和贸易中心，而且事实上新加坡在科技和工业方面花的心思比服务业还多。现在新加坡不仅拥有制造业的四大支柱产业，即石化电子、机械制造、生物、医药；而且也是世界上第三大炼油中心和石化中心，同时还是世界上最大的石油钻井平台制造国。在谋篇布局方面，新加坡比香港的眼光要远得多、高得多，也深得多。

　　从这个角度来看，虽然我们也知道贸易进出口总是有起有伏，但其实香港现在的货物吞吐量甚至已经慢慢被深圳盐田港和上海下洋港所超越。香港在转口贸易上的优势处于下降，而不是上升趋势。而新加坡仍有自己的优势。那么，从整个情况来看，香港作为所谓的微型城市经济体，是小政府大社会，虽然经济有很多跌宕起伏，但直到现在来讲仍然是世界上最自由的经济体系。但是我们注意到了，1984 年到 2017 年香港有一个最重要的问题没有解决，那就是实体经济的空洞化。所谓的"前店后厂"其实是在两个大背景下产生的。第一，港英当局有 1997 年的回归大限，所以没有必要为香港的长久发展去做布局。第二，"前店后厂"是市场经济的自然流动。这种经济形式导致了科技创新产业的匮乏——这是香港非常重要的软肋。尽管 1997 年，香港第一届特区政府提议将香港发展成为"数码港"和"中药港"，但今天香港的数码港主要是物业和房地产，真正入驻的高新科技企业实际上并不多。香港的大学所培养的高新科技人才或者到新加坡就业，或者被富士康挖走，或者去了台湾和韩国。香港没有办法聚集人才。今天香港的人才聚集在哪里呢？聚集在金融、地产，除此之外就是地产、金融。

　　香港这样一个没有实体经济的自由经济体，其长久发展是有隐忧的。只剩下金融服务和旅游业是没有办法支撑一个经济体的可持续长久发展的。这是香港面对的隐忧之一，从这点来讲，新加坡的领跑优势显而易见。

　　接下来我想谈香港未来二十年发展的高度和限度。首先，一国两制五十年不变。这是邓小平生前讲的。我今天中午跟王赓武先生说，整场论坛频繁地出现两个伟人的名字：一个是邓小平，一个是李光耀。这也就是说，我们是站在前人对这两座城市的命运的前瞻的基础上来谈眼前、当下和未来的问题。五十年不变，现在还剩下三十年，邓小平先生说五十年之后也没有变的必要。但是事实上，变化是存在的。会有变化吗？答案是显然的，而且很显然，比如说经济上就存在变化。

从1997年到2016年，香港经济的发展仍然是呈向上的趋势。香港并没有出现大面积的失业。尽管有人买不起楼，尽管在阶层固化的情况之下很难拥有七、八十年代中产阶级形成之初那样的社会流动性，尽管向上流动的管道受到更多的阻塞，但是就业空间和就业率并没有受到根本性的影响。买不起楼不等于一定要"上街"，虽然我也很希望在金钟打边炉——这也是我的香港梦。但从实际来讲，我们不能撇开法治框架去谈论政治意识问题和年轻人的政治参与问题。

从经济情况来看，香港现在所谓的四个主要行业中，物流和贸易实际上是在递减；旅游业虽然还可以，但是并不如我们所想象的那么畅旺。专业性服务和其他生产性服务则不尽人意，其中就包括会计、律师等行业。而香港所谓的六大优势行业，实际上并不具有难以取代的优势。虽然香港有六所优秀的大学，虽然也有创新科技产业，但是都不能形成拳头产品，不能形成独一无二的优势。这是香港目前要面对的问题。那么从行业增长所占的 GDP 比重来看，你会发现香港产业结构的固化很明显，没有新的产业进入，没有新的产业升级，持平发展，而支柱产业也并不如我们所想的那样有突飞猛进的变化。

关于五十年不变承诺下的香港变迁，这里不谈太多。我们可以看到，这几届香港特首的民意调查指数跌宕起伏。人们现在还可以对特首挑剔和批评，这也是香港现在很难得的一种自由。这一方面说明市民对政府的满意度有很多变化，同时也说明香港在九七之后，政治意识的苏醒、参与度的表现呈现多样化。而这种多样化其实给今天香港的 "一国两制" 也带来了显而易见的挑战，比如长达七十九天，占据了整条金融街的"占中"事件。这个事件比北京八九年六四运动的时间还长了两到三倍。这说明香港在法治社会基础上是可以承载这类政治压力的。它还能够把这样一种突如其来的爆发性民粹化的政治参与表现有序地、不完全失控地缓解和消化掉，这一点也不容易。

上世纪八十年代，中国政府在处理香港主权回归方案时，曾赋予它三个战略目标：第一，垂范台湾；第二，开放管道；第三，资金来源。时过境迁，二十年之后，我们再也听不到垂范台湾这样的诉求。回归前的后过渡期，中国大陆相对封闭，改革开放刚刚开始。香港的的确确扮演着开放管道的角色。大陆通过香港这个畅通无阻的管道可以走向世界，同时世界各国也通过香港走进中国大陆。但是这条管道现在变得不是那么的举足轻重了。现在大陆沿海经济发达地区的一个村长就可以带着很多人出国考察，大陆已经不再需要通过香港来进行这样的对外交往。

中国大陆现在是世界第二大经济体，外汇储备全世界第一。国家领导人整天发愁这钱怎么花。就资金来源而言，香港的优势只存在于优质资源的再分配，因为香港作为金融中心在提供优质服务方面功能尚在。但是大陆不再需要香港的资金。这三个所谓的战略目标基本上已经消失或者削弱。那么香港怎么办？这里面还包括上世纪八十年代之初，中国领导人对香港这座城市的定位有一些误判，比如说"马照跑，舞照跳"，其实当时是把香港作为一个经济城市来定位的。挣钱就行，其他的不要管。当时的中央政府忘记了任何殖民地或者经济体回归到宗主国的过程中，还有去殖民化这个任务远没有完成。香港居民的政治参与意识的苏醒，以及他们在"港人治港，高度自治"的基本法的规定之下对自身命运和参与香港社会度的表达越来越具有张力。

我们看到今天回归一代的政治参与意识十分高涨。最极端的就是那些鼓吹"港独"的人。今天上午香港中文大学还张贴着鼓吹"港独"的标语。回归已经二十年了，为什么会出现"港独"的诉求？或者说存在显而易见的疏离感。香港特区政府在殖民地回归以后的教育，尤其是认同教育是有问题的，其所产生的"恶果"，实质上跟台湾的李登辉、陈水扁政府所实行的"去中国化"教育的结果是一样的。这就使得殖民地回归以后的重新认同，出现了一代人的空白或者相对空白。这一代年轻人在成长过程中每天在报纸上看到的都是那些贪官污吏，而且这些内地的贪官污吏越贪越多。你说这些接受了西方教育价值观的香港孩子如何能对这样的社会现象、文化和价值体系产生认同呢？这就是今天二十年之后政治变迁之下，香港社会的新形态。我们对这样的政治参与意识的苏醒和爆发式增长，以及突然出现的、具有街头"暴民政治"表现还不适应，因此也不可能有正确和准确的判断。虽然习近平先生今年也说了"求大同，存大异"，但是不是每个人、每个部门领导人都有这种想法就要另当别论了。

对香港在中国现代化经济发展中的作用影响最大的是深圳的崛起。"东方之珠"的夜景很漂亮，但是深圳今天的夜景不会比东方之珠逊色。深圳的 GDP 总量已经快赶上香港，甚至超越香港。深圳的高新科技产业布局、创业氛围和器材也远远超过香港。深港一体化的大前提已经具备了。

中国其他一线城市的 GDP 也在飞速增长。香港并没有表现出应该有的优势。我们现在要谈的是未来。我这里要强调的是未来二十年。未来二十年，我们有很多的展望。我们已经看到了香港在中国整个架构之下的地位在逐渐改变；看到了香港的经济优势和它邻近几个地区的发展变化；看到了深圳、广东跟香港的变化；看到了北上广深等中心城市的变化；看到了曾经赋予香港的三个战略目标的变化。同时，我们也在展望。李光耀先生在 1996 年说过，香港需要一个有主见和坚定的行政首长，有廉洁和富有效率的公务员的协助，维持英国制度、法制以及合约的庄严，公平的商业原则以及公平竞争环境等优点。二十年后的今天，反思李光耀先生在 1996 年所说的这些话，李先生所讲的这些优点都还在吗？

有主见和坚定的行政首长是不是已经出来呢？廉洁且富有效率的公务员，这个体制是不是有一些异化呢？所谓的英国制度，也就是香港维持的最高效的法制的廉洁的制度，以及契约精神有没有受到削减？公平的商业原则和公平竞争的环境有没有变化呢？华润董事长宋林因为贪污渎职受审，而他同时也担任着香港廉政公署道德委员会主席。这样的差异性表现告诉了我们什么呢？我们一方面看到了香港法律所维持的尊严：我们把犯了过失、触犯了法律的曾荫权判刑了，把政务司司长锒铛入狱了。我们也看到了香港法律对那些在立法会没有遵守游戏规则的人给予了公正的判决。我们看到了香港法治精神的一脉相承，但我们有没有看到这里面也有出现某种程度的变化呢？当然有。1997 年回归之后的最初三年，在 "一国两制" 的框架下，大陆科长以上的干部禁止进入香港。但今天呢，某个触犯了大陆法律的商人可以从香港被带走，可以出现像二楼书店这样的事情。一般的香港人虽然不了解其中的缘由，但是他们对香港法治精神能否受到尊重和保护会有隐忧。

我觉得香港不管怎么变化，它没有办法改变其中华人民共和国特别行政区的性质。中国的快速崛起在很大程度上改变了两制之间的关系，改变了香港跟深圳和广东、香港跟南中国、香港跟整个中国之间的关系。香港 "一国两制" 成功与否，其实不再只是香港人自己的努力，而是取决于整个中国这个母体走向现代化的成功。有一种观点认为，"一国两制" 并不是先进制度和落后制度的联姻，而是两种不同制度之间的互容互通。从对制度的理解方面来看，香港可能更应该被视为大陆与世界沟通的桥梁，而不应该简单地认为社会主义是落后的，认为落后的社会主义拖了香港的后腿。这种说法有问题，因为它离开了上世纪八十年代中国共产党用 "一国两制" 的方式解决香港主权回归的大背景。那个时候的中国是贫穷的，是落后的，对香港、台湾、澳门和海外华人没有一点吸引力。所以，它当时很实事求是地面对了这个现象，实施了"一国两制"，解决了一个历史问题。这是中国共产党第一次对国际社会做出的承诺。它得到了国际社会的广泛认同。这里面当然也有整个时代的局限性，但是在确保主权归属毋庸置疑的前提之下，"一国两制"是对两种不同社会制度差异性的现实状况的一种实事求是的认定，是对两种社会制度存在明显差异性的现实尊重，是对先进发达的资本主义和相对落后的中国内地之间存在明显差异，尤其是政治、文明差异的这一事实的尊重。

首先，我认为这是中国共产党建立以来最令人值得肯定的一种时代进步，是中国治理者前所未有的面向国际社会的承诺。第二，改革开放四十年，中国有钱了，贪污起来都是几百亿的。经济上有了长足的进步。世界各地，大街小巷走到哪都能看到中国的游客。在法国巴黎，你可以看到中国游客一个人买十几个 LV，大呼小叫地走在大街上。这很令人感慨，我们这一代人经历过饥饿。经过近四十年的改革开放，多数人实现了小康，是来之不易的。但是你必须承认，在法治、廉政、价值观、意识形态等方面，中国跟外面的世界还是有着明显的差别。这构成了母体跟子体之间因客观差异性而产现的矛盾，而这个矛盾还会长期存在下去。五十年之后，只要香港不被"阴干"，不成为深圳的一个区。这种矛盾很有可能会继续存在。

香港在未来二十年跟内地的经济互动联系会更加的紧密。香港所扮演的角色将跟过去二十年完全不一样，它将不再是独一无二的经济引领者，其角色功能正在区域化，这点可以从大湾区的发展中看出来。政府的中央工作报告很明确地提出，大湾区是为了香港和澳门的发展着想。在"9+2"概念中，虽然中央政府设有 4 个直辖市和 5 个自治区，但香港和澳门特别行政区是重点地区。那么，在这样的一个过程中，香港在某些领域的独特优势会减弱，有些优势会增强，有些则会受到限制。比如基本法的二十三条立法以后要不要进入立法议程，进入立法议程以后香港社会各界会如何面对。关于香港的政治安全和国防安全，香港的 "政治异见人士" 又会如何面对，这些都是需要去注意的。在可预见的历史时期内，香港不可能改变它作为中华人民共和国特别行政区的性质。这在未来的二十年，甚至更长的时间内，都是没有办法突破的高度。个别人企图搞"港独"，难以形成气候。

台湾某位政要曾经给我看过一份美国中央情报局的研究报告，这份报告详细列举了台湾独立的三十二种可能性。美国对台湾问题研究得很透，根据这份研究，三十二种"台独"可能性只有一个共同的前提，那就是中国大陆要同意。这不仅是它的高度，也是它的限度。即便中国大陆的政治形势发生了无法估测的重大变动，这个高度和限度仍然不可逾越，也不必在争取逾越上做出不切实际的期望和想象。香港会逐渐变成中国的全球化城市，跟深圳、广东此消彼涨。从转口贸易到超级联系人，如果香港这个联系人的态度不好，生意也不容易做。

我要强调的是这样的高度和限度其实也就规定了香港在未来二十年、三十年跟新加坡的合作、交流与互动的高度和限度。未来二十年香港扮演什么角色？

首先，香港将是中国走向文明现代，即在法制、廉政、企业精神和公平竞争方面的参照系。香港所扮演的参照系角色只会加强，不会减弱。第二，是马马虎虎爱国主义的典范。现在强调的是爱国爱港。廖承志先生在生前曾严厉批评统战工作人士，海外华人、台港澳同胞一定要爱国。爱国并不等于爱党，马马虎虎就行。什么叫马马虎虎。我是中国人，我希望中华民族富强。行了，这样你就是个伟大的爱国者了。这才叫做最广泛的统一战线。敌人少少的，朋友多多的。毛泽东说，政治工作就是要这样搞的。

习近平先生强调的是，求大同，存大异。"一国两制"是大异和大同的结合。但是不是人人都有这样的雅量？这样的情怀？这样的眼光？只是一个习近平显然是不够的。

最后一点，政治参与和民主化进程的先试先行。无论是有序的民主，程序化的民主或者实质性的民主，香港都有条件去先试先行。即便在这个过程中出现了民粹化，出现了港独，出现了暴民政治、街头政治，我觉得这都是中国走向现代化文明的一个参照系。它可能是经验，也可能是教训。我不清楚有没有人讨论香港在未来所扮演这样的角色，但我认为这样一个角色是存在的。

下面来谈未来二十年的想象。从实际上来讲，香港和新加坡在未来二十年的想像空间要比前二十年、前四十年、前六十年多得多。虽然会受到国际社会彼此间竞争的影响，但两者的伙伴关系会继续存在。香港仍然是新加坡的一个"假想敌"。政治形态差异决定了这两座城市没有办法恢复曾经的互动水准。两者的关系会受到更多不确定因素的制约，比如国际形势、亚太局势和大陆的影响。香港要保持东方之珠的基本特质，就要保持原有的社会制度，保持廉洁高效的公务员协助，保持像李光耀先生生前所期待的那样。 如果香港提前完成改变，成为众多中国城市之一，那么它跟新加坡之间的双城记无须再说下去了。那时，新加坡要挑选上海、广州或者深圳去做另外一个比较。

如果香港现在所有的特色被"阴干"，即如金耀基先生所说，被边缘化，或者整个竞争力萎顿了，那我们可以说，一个被"阴干"的香港，不是中国领导人所乐见的。我相信这也不是新加坡人所乐见的。

在这里，我引用一句话。这句话出自厦门大学台湾研究所研究院院长刘国深。他谈到台湾问题的时候说：台湾问题的终极解药是大陆自身的发展。他指出，大陆一定要清楚，台湾人对共产党、对大陆的制度有恐惧感和不信任感，这是客观现实。台湾问题的终极解药是大陆的自身发展。请把这句话里的"台湾"改成"香港"，把"法理台独"改成"法理港独"，道理是一样的。

Singapore and Hong Kong:

Twins Basking in a Chinese Presence

FENG Da Hsuan

Professor FENG Da Hsuan is the Chief Advisor of China's Silk Road iValley Research Institute, the 6th largest and influential think-tank of China. Trained as a theoretical physicist, he has in the past several years been deeply engaging in various aspects of the Belt and Road Initiative (BRI) and has given major speeches worldwide about this issue. Professor Feng is a well-known theoretical physicist and the former Vice President for Research of the University of Texas at Dallas. He is the author of the book *Edu-renaissance: Notes from a Globetrotting Higher Educator*, published by World Scientific Publishing Co. Pte. Ltd.

I am deeply grateful to have the opportunity to attend this workshop of profound importance in East Asia. Thinking back, almost from the start, my life has, in one way or another, revolved around Hong Kong and Singapore. I spent my formative years in Singapore, and as the old cliché says, "before Singapore was Singapore!" In the past ten years while living in Asia, I renewed many of my interactions with these two cities. Certainly, in the past three years in Macau, its proximity to Hong Kong has allowed me to gain a deeper, if not profound, understanding of that city. In this sense, I am emotionally tied to both in a palpable manner.

I am not a social scientist, nor a historian, and certainly not an economist. I am merely a theoretical physicist by training. However, in one way or another, my life seems to revolve around the Asia Pacific, even when I was in the United States. So, my discussion today centers on some of my personal observations of Hong Kong and Singapore basking in a Chinese presence.

As Hong Kong is legally part of China, it is *not* a country but a city under "One Country, Two Systems" (OCTS). Singapore, however, is a country. To avoid political incorrectness, I shall, for the rest of the discussion when the need arises, refer to them collectively as "the two cities."

Dear friends, I hope you can agree with me that it would be a colossal mistake to discuss Singapore and Hong Kong without discussing China's impact on the two of them. To discuss the future of the two cities and not take into account the profound influence of China, is akin to two people having a conversation in a room and not paying attention to the enormous presence of an elephant. This is especially so because China was transformative in the past two decades.

I left Singapore in 1964 for the United States, carrying a Malaysian passport. That year, in my dormitory room, I heard the news that China had become a nuclear power. As my major was physics, I naturally became excited. I have to admit that I did not fully appreciate what having nuclear power really meant. My true understanding of China came eight years later when I became a postdoc in the Department of Theoretical Physics in the University of Manchester. In the Departmental Library, I saw for the first time the journal *Chinese Journal of Physics*! I remember I was exhilarated at that moment because I saw high level physics discussed in Chinese. To this date, I remember an article by Academician He Zou-Xiu (何祚庥) on particle physics. I visited China in 1981 for the first time after the Communists took over in 1949. Since then, I made over 200 visits until I came back to Asia in 2007. After which, my interactions blossomed into a multitude of areas and I lost count as to how many times I visited the Mainland.

You may ask, why only China? After all, during my formative years in Singapore, I could palpably feel the presence of the United States in the region. I am sure that was true for Hong Kong as well. Furthermore, both Hong Kong and Singapore were British Colonies for well over one and a half centuries.

The reason why I singled out China's influence and impact is because until fairly recently, for sure as recent as "China's Reform and Opening Up" (中国改革开放) of 1976, or maybe as late as the beginning of the 21st century, because of its conditions, China's impact on Singapore was not comparable to the west. For Hong Kong, because it was adjacent to China, the influence was palpable. Yet, for both cities, China's economic and social impact were not felt until the end of the 20th century and the start of the 21st century, especially when China began the so-called Peaceful Rise (和平崛起). I think it is safe to say that unlike the United States (US) and United Kingdom (UK), where both had influence in these two cities that are long and longer, China's is recent.

As far as the Peaceful Rise (和平崛起) of China is concerned, I think it is worth pointing out that during the Ming Dynasty, Admiral Zheng He led a mighty armada, which included hundreds of ships and nearly thirty thousand soldiers all across Southeast Asia, South Asia (even Mecca because he was a Moslem) and West Africa. Yet not one inch of land became a Chinese colony. I wonder whether the concept of colonisation, unlike the European nations, was in the Chinese DNA?

Although GDP is not a panacea economic indicator, it nevertheless gives us a sense of the movement. The importance of China for Singapore and Hong Kong can be seen from their historical GDPs.

Table 1.   GDP figures of Hong Kong, Singapore and China in 1983, 1997 and 2017

GDP (in Billion US$)	1983	1997	2017
Hong Kong	30	177	332
Singapore	18	100	291
China	308	965	11800

Source: Knoema Corporation, data available online at knoema. com (accessed on December 1, 2017).

From 1997 to 2017, the GDP figures of Hong Kong and Singapore grew nearly 2 and 3 times respectively, while China grew more than

12 times. In fact, Singapore's and Hong Kong's growth are closer to that of the United States (2.3 times) than China. This I believe is a signal that the two cities have reached the "developed" stage while China remains a "developing" country. In 2014, Xi Jinping declared at the United Nations that:

> "We will strive for the peaceful development of the world, but China is still a developing country, and its responsibilities should be commensurate with its status."

Another truly fascinating aspect is that in 1983, when Deng Xiao Ping and Margaret Thatcher began their OCTS negotiation, Hong Kong's GDP was one-tenth of China's. How that played in the OCTS negotiation is a fascinating question. I often say that in the past three decades, "China has experienced a three centuries' worth of growth!" The rapid rise of China's GDP since 1997 is surely one of the reasons why China's presence is so palpable, not only in relation to the two cities, but the world as well.

What I am trying to say is that China's discernable impact on the two cities happened essentially in the last 20 years, its impact time derivative is much larger than that of the US and UK. As a result, the time for the people of both cities to adjust to China's enormous, "almost instant" presence was short as well. Before one knew it, China's economic and social impact on both cities were here! It is safe to say that not only people from the two cities, but the world at large, did not expect China, a nation with the largest population in the world, to rise with such dizzying speed.

Singapore and Hong Kong in the Past Twenty Years

As we can see, on 1 July 2017, Hong Kong which was under British colonial rule for some 150 years celebrated the 20th year anniversary of its return to China. Such a return was, and still is, absolutely unprecedented, since Hong Kong has operated under the auspices of OCTS. Like Hong Kong, Singapore was also a British colony for a century. Although the British were "gone," you can still feel their presence. Both HK's current and past Chief Executives, Carrie Lam and C. Y. Leung received their advanced education in the UK. This is also true of Singapore, whose

Prime Ministers Lee Kuan Yew and Lee Hsien Loong are Cambridge educated.

In the past twenty years, there is one aspect which made the people of Singapore and Hong Kong profoundly different. People from Singapore are unabashedly Singaporeans. Singaporeans with Chinese heritage is simply just that. Hong Kong's citizens are legally Chinese citizens. Yet because of OCTS, some have "split loyalties."

It is equally interesting that although it was in 1965, fifty-two years ago, that Singapore became an independent country with all the attributions pertaining to it, it was in 2015 when Lee Kuan Yew passed away that Singapore's governance entered a new era.

I think it is fair to say that in 1965, it was the political wisdom of Lee Kuan Yew and his team of compatriots (such as Toh Chin Chye, Goh Keng Swee and so on) who made Singapore what it is today, a miracle of Asia. Of course, Asia and the world in 2017 bear no resemblance to Asia and the world in 1965. This means that Singapore's new generation of leaders must today have equal but different wisdom from their 1965 predecessors.

Two months ago, I was fortunate to be in the audience to witness the dialogue between my friend Robin Hu and Premier Lee Hsien-Loong. From Lee's body and spoken language, coupled with his quick wit, I saw in action the new generation of leadership. When Robin asked Premier Lee what he thought about "small countries' foreign policies", Lee answered with the following:

"We work on the basis that the world will progress, countries will prosper and our roles will have to change as they grow more prosperous, more capable, and more open to the world. What we used to do and what they used to find us useful for will change. You cannot sell the old medicines to a patient who is in a new situation or who no longer needs medicines. Therefore, we must be able to move ahead with the world and as others make progress, we continue to make progress with them and in some aspects, ahead of them and we remain useful to them. So you look at our projects in China. There are three G-to-G projects but they are not the same."

Hong Kong became self-governing under the auspices of OCTS in 1997. Its leadership had to climb the steep political learning curve, especially how to interact with the Mainland. Just like Singapore's leaders, Hong Kong's current leaders also need to be different and adjust to the current social, economic and political ambience.

The new Chief Executive of Hong Kong, Carrie Lam, in a speech delivered on 7 July this year:

> "Capitalising on our unique advantages under the principle (of OCTS), we have thrived as a vibrant international metropolitan city. With the authorisation by the Central People's Government for Hong Kong to conduct our external affairs, we have consolidated and expanded our vast connections with countries and regions around the globe and across different fields, including trade, investment, finance, aviation, culture, and legal co-operation."

By adhering to these guidelines to propel Singapore and Hong Kong forward, *vis-à-vis* China, I see that there is no reason not to be confident that these new leaders can manifest new and different wisdom to propel the cities in the unchartered and turbulent waters of the Asia Pacific in the 21st century.

Finale

It is probably not an exaggeration to say that China today is not the same as the China of 1997. I am confident that compared to China in 1976, the difference is not measured in decades but centuries.

The following are GDP charts for the world's top ten countries in 1983 (the year Deng Xiao Ping began negotiations with Margaret Thatcher), 1997 (the year Hong Kong's sovereignty returned to China) and 2014.

From these three tables, between 1983 and 1997, China changed only from 8th to 7th position. However, in 2014, it catapulted to become the 2nd largest economy in the world.

In my opinion, the biggest change of China is that its wealth is beginning to penetrate into the general population. According to the founder of Alibaba, Jack Ma (马云), there are some three hundred million "middle class" Chinese today. This is stunning because this number is comparable to the entire US population (not just the US middle class population). It

Table 2.   GDP Chart (1983)

1		United States	3,508,800,060,000
2		Japan	1,182,300,240,000
3		Germany	745,801,580,000
4		France	547,915,137,000
5		United Kingdom	459,258,757,000
6		Italy	426,865,000,000
7		Canada	333,808,828,000
8		China	227,375,481,000
9		India	215,169,253,000
10		Brazil	203,304,518,000

Source: Ranking of the World's Richest Countries by GDP, data available online at http://en.classora.com/reports/t24369/general/ranking-of-the-worlds-richest-countries-by-gdp?edition=1983&fields= (accessed on 1 Dec, 2017)

also means that there is now a very large number of Chinese who have disposable income. No doubt, any time you have such a large group of middle class people, if entrepreneurs can find common interest in them, it becomes a business.

Let me give you an interesting example. We all know that the "king of fruits", i.e. durians, are dear to the hearts of Southeast Asian people. For years, the price of durians was relatively stable. Yet suddenly in the past

Table 3.   GDP Chart (1997)

1		United States	8,250,900,100,000
2		Japan	4,258,577,250,000
3		Germany	2,160,590,980,000
4		France	1,424,378,040,000
5		United Kingdom	1,328,084,420,000
6		Italy	1,192,322,140,000
7		China	952,652,660,000
8		Brazil	871,200,000,000
9		Canada	637,536,500,000
10		Spain	572,637,510,000

Source: Ranking of the World's Richest Countries by GDP, data available online at http://en.classora.com/reports/t24369/general/ranking-of-the-worlds-richest-countries-by-gdp?edition=1997&fields= (accessed on 1 Dec, 2017)

several years, the price spiked. The reason was because the Chinese in the coastal provinces, Guangdong, Fujian and a few others developed a genuine love for the taste of durian. I was told that Chinese love durian mooncakes. In fact, even Chinese as far north as Jilin Province are catching on to this fad. Obviously, when you have hundreds of millions of people liking a certain commodity, in this case, the durian, you have a real market.

Another interesting example is that the Chinese in the last five to six years made enormous gains in what Haiming Liang and I refer to as the "omnipresent economy"(OE). In a nut shell, OE is the economy that

Table 4.   GDP Chart (2014)

1		**United States**	17,419,000,100,000
2		**China**	10,360,104,900,000
3		**Japan**	4,601,461,300,000
4		**Germany**	3,852,556,040,000
5		**United Kingdom**	2,941,885,610,000
6		**France**	2,829,192,000,000
7		**Brazil**	2,346,118,280,000
8		**Italy**	2,144,338,180,000
9		**India**	2,066,902,420,000
10		**Russia**	1,860,597,970,000

Source: Ranking of the World's Richest Countries by GDP, data available online at http://en.classora.com/reports/t24369/general/ranking-of-the-worlds-richest-countries-by-gdp?edition=2014&fields= (accessed on 1 Dec, 2017)

springs out by combining mobile internet and smart devices. In 2005, Thomas Friedman stated that "the world is flat". Yet, by 2010, when he wrote the second book, when social media such as Facebook became ubiquitous, the world had become "flatter". What is truly amazing is that by 2017, China's effort in flattening at least China further is breathtaking. In China today, the entire economy, from the most sophisticated cities, such as Shanghai, to the most remote rural regions, OE has taken over.

Finally, in 2013, President Xi Jinping announced to the world the "Belt and Road Initiative" (BRI). Never before in the history of mankind, has it been that a nation of such magnitude intends to co-develop, however arduous, with people of different civilizations and ways and means. Such an action, I think, should and probably would propel people involved in BRI, and Hong Kong and Singapore are surely not the exceptions, to truly learn about China, its culture, and ways and means, and vice versa.

Ultimately, what is truly impressive about China currently is not merely its breathtaking economic growth. What is impressive is how the economic growth has impacted the Chinese mindset. Today, there are, within China, more and more conversations about how it can open up to the outside world. Understanding this mindset, whether you are from Hong Kong, Singapore, or elsewhere, will be absolutely critical in establishing a relationship, business or otherwise, with China.